U.S. ★★★
CITIZENSHIP
A Step-by-Step Guide

2nd Edition

New York

Library of Congress Cataloging-in-Publication Data:
U.S. citizenship : a step-by-step guide.—2nd ed. / by LearningExpress, LLC.
  p. cm.
  Rev. ed. of: U.S. citizenship / Felice Primeau Devine. c2001.
  ISBN: 978-1-57685-577-5
1. Citizenship—United States—Handbooks, manuals, etc. 2. Naturalization—
United States—Handbooks, manuals, etc. 3. Americanization—Handbooks,
manuals, etc. I. Devine, Felice Primeau. U.S. citizenship. II. LearningExpress
(Organization) III. Title: US citizenship.
JK1758.D48 2007
323.6'230973—dc22

                                                                    2006036559

Printed in the United States of America

9 8 7 6 5 4 3 2

Second Edition

ISBN: 978-1-57685-577-5

For information on LearningExpress, other LearningExpress products, or bulk
sales, please write to us at:
    LearningExpress
    55 Broadway
    8th Floor
    New York, NY 10006

Or visit us at:
    www.learnatest.com

CONTENTS

INTRODUCTION

How to Use This Book

Congratulations—you've decided to become a U.S. citizen! While you've been thinking about whether or not to seek citizenship, you have no doubt realized that this is a big decision. This decision comes with some very important responsibilities. But before you can realize these responsibilities and show your commitment to the U.S. Constitution and the American people, you first have to go through naturalization— the process by which immigrants become citizens.

Don't give up yet! Yes, naturalization is a complex process. There are applications to complete, interviews to attend, and tests to take. With a little step-by-step guidance, however, your naturalization can be as easy as American pie!

Did You Know . . .

. . . that more than 10% of the U.S. population is foreign born? This means that you are not alone in deciding to become a U.S. citizen. In fact, the United States is a country made up of immigrants; when you become a citizen, you will be following in the footsteps of millions of Americans.

It All Starts Here

This book will provide you with the basic information, rules, and regulations you need to know to become a U.S. citizen. It is not intended to serve as a substitute for legal guidance. For information on resources for legal guidance, see Appendix B.

In Chapter 1, you will be introduced to all of the steps involved in naturalization. This chapter includes a timeline that will allow you to easily keep track of where you are in the process and where to go next.

> ☆ **NATURALIZATION:** the process of conferring the
> rights of a national on; especially: to admit to
> citizenship

Chapter 2 covers how people qualify for citizenship and the eligibility requirements for naturalization (one of the four ways to qualify for citizenship). This information can be confusing for applicants, so we've made the process simple by using the steps outlined in this book. This chapter will explain exactly how to determine if you meet the naturalization requirements. It also will discuss where to go for additional legal help, if you need it.

> ☆ **ELIGIBILITY:** the state of being qualified to participate
> or be chosen: entitlement

Chapter 3 will provide you with details on the steps for applying for citizenship. You'll learn what documents are necessary, see a sample application, and gain general familiarity with the naturalization process.

Did You Know . . .

> . . . that only U.S. citizens have the right to vote? (With a green card, you can live, work, or go to school in the United States, but you *cannot* vote for elected officials.)

Chapter 4 covers the most important element of naturalization—the U.S. Citizenship Exam. In this chapter, you'll find an overview of the exam—what to expect and how to prepare. You'll learn invaluable study tips and how to deal with test anxiety. After this introduction, you'll be ready to test yourself with official U.S. Citizenship and Immigration Services (USCIS) questions in Chapter 6.

As you will see from the sample questions, studying U.S. civics will be a main focus during your preparation. A quick review of U.S. civics—including history, government, general civics, and important information on the U.S. Constitution—is contained in Chapter 6.

Special situations and exceptions, such as dual citizenship and marriage visas, are covered in Chapter 7. Please note that this book does not contain legal advice, but it will provide you with the background information and rules to follow during the naturalization process.

We have included lots of resources to help make your naturalization process run smoothly: Appendix A contains a directory of USCIS offices all over the country. Appendix B is a selective list of resources to make your preparation easier. Appendix C contains sample forms, and Appendix D is a list of government acronyms and abbreviations that are sometimes hard to understand.

The Outlook on Immigration

In the summer of 2001, President George W. Bush visited Ellis Island, the New York port where over 12 million immigrants have arrived over the years. As you will discover in the following chapters, becoming a citizen can take a long time. Promising to accelerate—or speed up—the immigration process, President Bush welcomed 29 new citizens to the United States at their Oath Ceremony on historic Ellis Island. He said, "Immigration is not a problem to be solved, it is a sign of a confident and successful nation . . . New arrivals should be greeted not with suspicion and resentment, but with openness and courtesy."

Source: The *New York Times.* Tuesday, July 10, 2001

With the right preparation, you soon will find yourself reciting the Oath of Allegiance to the United States of America at your swearing-in ceremony!

CHAPTER 1

Naturalization— An Overview of the Process of Becoming a Citizen

IN 2004, ALMOST 540,000 people were naturalized as U.S. citizens. They successfully completed the process that you are now beginning, probably with the help of friends, family, and resources like this book. If the process of becoming a U.S. citizen seems overwhelming at times, you can rest assured that hundreds of thousands of people are going through the process, too. And they, like you, know that if they are prepared, they will succeed.

The best way to be prepared is to know what to expect. This chapter will give you an overview of naturalization in the United States. It will tell you what you should do first and when, ultimately leading to the day you become a citizen.

Did You Know . . .

. . . that the Hispanic population in the United States is largest in California, Florida, and Texas? According to July 2004 population estimates, Los Angeles County, California, with 4.6 million Latino residents, leads all counties nationwide in total Hispanic population. Dade County, Florida, which includes Miami and has 1.4 million Latinos, was a distant second to Los Angeles County. Harris County, Texas, which includes Houston, was third with 1.3 million Hispanics.

Source: Bernstein, Robert. "Texas Becomes Nation's Newest 'Majority-Minority' State, Census Bureau Announces." U.S. Census Bureau News, Washington, D.C. Aug. 11, 2005

Step 1

Determine your eligibility. In general, you will meet the eligibility requirements if one of the following applies to you:

◆ You have been a lawful, permanent resident for at least five years, OR
◆ You have been a lawful, permanent resident for at least three years and have been married to a U.S. citizen for those three years, AND
◆ You have been physically present in the United States for at least half of the time that you have been a lawful permanent resident (30 or 18 months).

In addition, you may be eligible if:

◆ You are a lawful permanent resident child of U.S. citizen parent(s).
◆ You have qualifying military service in the Armed Forces of the United States. (Forms N-426 and G-325B are required in addition to Form N-400.)

This will be discussed further in Chapter 2.

☆ **GREEN CARD:** an identity card attesting the permanent resident status of an alien in the United States

Step 2

Obtain a Form N-400 from the U.S. Citizenship and Immigration Services (USCIS). This form is your Application for Naturalization. To obtain this form, you can contact your local USCIS office, visit the USCIS website at www.uscis.gov/graphics/formsfee/forms/index.htm, or call 1-800-870-FORM.

Step 3

Gather your application material and send it to the USCIS with the appropriate application fee and supporting documents. You can file your application up to three months in advance of your actual eligibility date.
   Your application will consist of:

♦ Form N-400
♦ The filing fee of $330 and fingerprint fee of $70. These fees may be paid in one check totaling $400, payable to the U.S. Citizenship and Immigration Services. (Please confirm fees with the USCIS before you send any money; this was the correct price at time of publication.)
♦ Three color photographs, 2″× 2″ (You can get these pictures taken anywhere that makes passport photos.)
♦ A photocopy of the front and back of your green card

Step 4

Get your fingerprints taken. This step is taken *after* you submit your application. After the USCIS receives your complete application packet, it will send you a fingerprint appointment letter. This letter will contain information about when and where to go to get your fingerprints taken. (The USCIS has established Application Support Centers in most metropolitan areas, as well as mobile fingerprinting vans to facilitate fingerprinting.) Read and follow the instructions in the letter carefully. Also, make sure to take the letter with you to your fingerprint appointment.

You may be wondering why you have to be fingerprinted. The Federal Bureau of Investigations (FBI) will use your fingerprints to run a criminal background check on you. This is one way of ensuring that you fulfill the good moral character requirement, which you'll learn about in the next chapter.

Step 5

Study, study, study! You have completed all of the steps for filing your application. Now you can focus on learning more about U.S. history and government. You will be tested on these issues during your interview. It is important that you study because you must answer at least 70% of the questions correctly in order to pass. Chapters 5 and 6 provide you with sample questions and an overview of U.S. civics. Use these chapters, along with other books on how to pass the citizenship test, when you are preparing. A great preparation guide is LearningExpress's *Pass the U.S. Citizenship Exam, 2nd Edition.*

How, Where, and When to Study

You can successfully carry out your study plan by:

- ➤ Finding a quiet location
- ➤ Using good reading lights
- ➤ Turning off the radio and television
- ➤ Asking your family and friends for help
- ➤ Organizing a study group

Setting your study goals and writing down your study schedule will help you to master the material on your test if you follow these five steps.

Step 6

Attend your interview and oral exam. The USCIS will send you a letter telling you the date of your interview. Do not be surprised if this date is up to (or even well over) one year after you filed your application. Be prepared to provide updated information, such as changes of address and excursions outside of the United States, after filing your N-400 application.

When you attend your interview, be prepared to answer questions about your application, yourself, your family, your work, and your life in general. Be sure to honestly answer all the questions. Chapter 4 covers the interview process in greater detail.

Step 7

If you passed your interview and oral exam, this will be the last and most exciting step of the process. You will receive a letter from the USCIS telling you the date and time of your swearing-in ceremony. At the ceremony, you will take the Oath of Allegiance and receive your U.S. citizenship certificate.

There are two important things to remember while you are going through the process of becoming a U.S. citizen. First, *always be honest.* Answer all questions truthfully—do not lie about your situation, where you live, where you've worked, any criminal matters, nothing. Second, *always be prepared.* If you are filling out your Form N-400, gather all of the information you will need before you get started. Make a few copies of the form and practice filling it out properly and completely in order to prevent cross-outs and errors. If you are going to your interview, be sure you have spent adequate time studying U.S. history and civics.

Oath of Allegiance: If you pass your test and interview, you will recite this oath at your swearing-in ceremony:

> *I hereby declare, on oath, that I absolutely and entirely renounce and abjure all allegiance and fidelity to any foreign prince, potentate, state, or sovereignty of whom or which I have heretofore been a subject or citizen; that I will support and defend the Constitution and laws of the United States of America against all enemies, foreign and domestic; that I will bear true faith and allegiance to the same; that I will bear arms on behalf of the United States when required by the law; that I will perform noncombatant service in the Armed Forces*

of the United States when required by the law; that I will perform work of national importance under civilian direction when required by the law; and that I take this obligation freely without any mental reservation or purpose of evasion; so help me God.

☆ **ABJURE: to reject solemnly**
☆ **FIDELITY: the quality or state of being faithful**

What does the Oath of Allegiance mean? Well, first of all, it means that you are willing to leave behind your former identity as a citizen of your native country. This is a serious thing to do, and it's something that you need to consider thoroughly before starting your citizenship process. Secondly, when you pledge your allegiance to the United States, it means that you will do your share to support your new country no matter what—even if that means not supporting your native land. For some people, this is a very difficult thing to do. Make sure that you are ready and prepared to honor this part of the oath. Sometimes, this oath will mean that you need to support the United States of America in a war—either through combat, active duty, or civilian work at home. And, under certain special circumstances, you may be called on to do some work of "national importance" on behalf of the United States, based on your national origin or special skills. The most important thing is to understand what you are pledging yourself to and to be willing to take this oath without hesitation. To help you understand more about your new country, read the U.S. Constitution and Declaration of Independence, both found in Chapter 6.

Now that you have an overview of the naturalization process, let's read on about *eligibility requirements* for U.S. citizenship in the next chapter.

☆ ☆ ☆

MIGUEL'S STORY

I WAS 16 years old when my family and I left Colombia for the United States. When we first arrived in New York, it felt like I was in a movie. There were all different kinds of people on the street, just like I had imagined. Right then I knew I would like America very much. It didn't take me long to learn to speak English, and my English as a Second Language teacher in high school helped me very much.

When I entered the workforce I found that not being a citizen kept me from some career opportunities, so one day on the way home from my job as a doorman, I stopped at the New York Public Library and did some research on gaining citizenship. I was very torn about making the decision to become an American—I love my homeland of Colombia—but by then I had spent half my life in the United States, and I realized that if I were anywhere else in the world and somebody asked me where I was from, I would proudly tell them *America.* So, I made the decision to go for it. I found a couple of books in the library that helped me through the process, and my sister Daniela, who went through the naturalization process a few years earlier, was also a great help. I also discovered that there are many nonprofit organizations to assist candidates for naturalization with everything from legal help to studying for the interview test.

It is important to know that all the materials and helpful people will get you nowhere if you don't put 100% effort into the process of becoming a citizen. It is not particularly difficult, but there are many details and unfortunately much paperwork and waiting in lines, and it can be a very tedious process. It took about 16 months from the first time I contacted the USCIS to being sworn in as a citizen, but it varies according to each case. My advice would be to fill in the application neatly and with accurate information and use the waiting time to study for the exam in advance. Sixteen months seems like a long time, but it was within the estimated time given me by the USCIS. I didn't really know anything about American history so I needed that time to study. The part of the test that scared me the most was trying to remember the names of the nine Supreme Court Judges; my favorite part was learning the famous quotes by patriots of the Revolution. The more information you know regarding history, government, and economics is relevant for the test. When I was young I probably would have dreaded the studying, but I really enjoyed it—and it inspired me to read up on Colombian history, as well.

In the end, the oral interview was much easier than I thought, and the swearing-in ceremony was surprisingly solemn. I am very proud to be able to call myself an American.

☆ ☆ ☆

CHAPTER 2

Eligibility Requirements

DETERMINING ELIGIBILITY can be one of the most confusing parts of the naturalization process. It is also one of the most important steps. If you are not eligible for naturalization, *you cannot apply for citizenship*. This chapter will explain the eligibility requirements for naturalization. Several of the requirements can be confusing for applicants. These requirements will be covered in greater detail.

You must be at least 18 years old.

This requirement is clear cut. If you are younger than 18 years old, you are *not* eligible. You must wait until you turn 18 to apply for citizenship. However, children of U.S. citizens may be eligible to derive citizenship from their parent(s).

You must be a permanent resident of the United States, and have been issued a Permanent Resident Card (formerly called Alien Registration Card and commonly referred to as a green card).

If you have not been issued a Permanent Resident Card or *green card,* then you are not a permanent resident and cannot apply for citizenship. If you think you are a permanent resident but you have not been issued a Permanent Resident Card, you should contact your local USCIS office. Be sure that you followed the three steps to becoming a permanent resident properly.

You must have been a permanent resident for five years or more (three years if married to a U.S. citizen).

If you have been a permanent resident for more than five years, you are eligible. This means you hold a Permanent Resident Card. If you have been a permanent resident for a period of time between three and five years, you are eligible only if ALL of the following are true:

◆ You are married to and living with a U.S. citizen, AND
◆ You have been married to that U.S. citizen for the past three years, or more, AND
◆ Your spouse has been a U.S. citizen for at least three years, AND
◆ You have not been out of the country for 18 months or more in the last three years.

If all of the following are not true, and you have been a permanent resident for a period of time between three and five years, then you are not eligible.

If you have been a permanent resident for *fewer* than three years, you are not eligible. Also, filing taxes with the IRS as a "nonresident alien" provides the USCIS with a rebuttable presumption that you have "relinquished/abandoned" your permanent resident status, thus making you possibly ineligible.

During the last five years, you must NOT have been outside of the United States for 30 months or more.

Immigration lawyers and counselors claim that this is one of the most confusing requirements for their clients. Essentially, you are required to be physically present in the United States for at least half of the minimum time (five years) that you are required to be a permanent resident. You must be a permanent resident for at least five years, or 60 months. So, you must have been physically present in the United States for 30 months, or half of that time.

To determine whether or not you are eligible, gather your travel records from the past five years. Add up all of the time you spent out of the country. If it is less than 30 months, you are eligible. If the time you spent out of the country is greater than 30 months, your date of eligibility will be pushed back until you have been physically present for 30 months of the past five years.

Let's look at Maria's situation. She was granted permanent resident status on July 1, 2001. If she were not out of the country for more than 30 months between that day and June 30, 2006, she would be eligible on June 30, 2006. If, however, she traveled to her home country three times for a total of 32 months during that period, she would not be eligible on June 30, 2006.

Here's a simplification of how her date would move back:

July 1, 2001—permanent resident status granted
August 1, 2001–September 30, 2001—traveled outside the United States
February 1, 2002–July 31, 2002—traveled outside the United States
September 1, 2002–January 31, 2003—traveled outside the United States
January 1, 2004–July 31, 2004—traveled outside the United States
March 1, 2005–August 31, 2005—traveled outside the United States
December 1, 2005–January 31, 2006—traveled outside the United States

As of June 30, 2006 (five years as a permanent resident), her total time spent traveling outside of the United States = 28 months. Based on this travel, if Maria made no other trips outside the United States, she would be eligible on June 30, 2006.

Since becoming a permanent resident, you must not have taken a trip out of the United States that lasted for one year or more. (It is strongly recommended that trips outside the United States last for no longer than six months.)

If you travel, or have traveled, outside the United States for a period of one year or longer, you must have an approved "Application to Preserve Residence for Naturalization Purposes" (Form N-470). If not, you are ineligible.

Exceptions

It's great that the government offers the N-470 form to preserve your residency status if you need to leave the country. However, you can't count on this getting approved. With so many people applying for citizenship every year, the process gets harder and harder to complete early. Just keep in mind that if you leave the United States for more than six months, you may have to start over as you work toward getting five years of permanent residency.

You must have resided in the district or state in which you are applying for citizenship for the last three months.

There are no tricky calculations here. You simply must live in the district or state for three months. If you do not fulfill this requirement, you must wait until you do. While you are waiting, you can prepare your application so that it is ready once you have lived in your state or district for three months.

You must be able to read, write, and speak basic English.

There are three exceptions to this requirement. These may apply to you if:

◆ You are over age 50 and have lived in the United States for more than 20 years since becoming a permanent resident, OR
◆ You are over age 55 and have lived in the United States for more than 15 years since becoming a permanent resident, OR
◆ You have a disability preventing you from fulfilling this requirement. If this is true, you must file a "Medical Certification for Disability Exceptions" (Form N-648).

You must be able to pass the civics portion of the oral exam.

There are exceptions to this requirement, as well. These may apply to you if:

◆ You are over age 50 and have lived in the United States for more than 20 years since becoming a permanent resident, OR
◆ You are over age 55 and have lived in the United States for more than 15 years since becoming a permanent resident, OR
◆ You have a disability preventing you from fulfilling this requirement. If this is true, you must file a "Medical Certification for Disability Exceptions" (Form N-648).

Read Chapter 4 for more information on the language and civics section of the oral exam.

You must be a person of good moral character.

No exceptions here! If your moral character can be disputed, you probably are not eligible. You should note that it is not worth lying about your character and any crimes you may have committed. When you are fingerprinted, the FBI will use your prints to run a criminal background check on you.

> ☆ **MORAL CHARACTER:** one of the attributes or features that make up and distinguish an individual

See the following list of examples of things that would tarnish your good moral character.

Examples of Things That Might Show a Lack of Good Moral Character

- ◆ Any crime against a person with intent to harm
- ◆ Any crime against property or the government that involves "fraud" or evil intent
- ◆ Two or more crimes for which the aggregate sentence was five years or more
- ◆ Violating any controlled-substance law of the United States, any state, or any foreign country
- ◆ Habitual drunkenness or drunk driving
- ◆ Illegal gambling
- ◆ Prostitution
- ◆ Polygamy (marriage to more than one person at the same time)
- ◆ Lying to gain immigration benefits
- ◆ Failing to pay court-ordered child support or alimony payments
- ◆ Confinement in jail, prison, or similar institution for which the total confinement was 180 days or more during the past five years (three years if you are applying based on your marriage to a U.S. citizen)
- ◆ Failing to complete any probation, parole, or suspended sentence before you apply for naturalization
- ◆ If you have recently been ordered deported or removed, you are not eligible for citizenship. If you are in removal proceedings, you may not apply for citizenship until the proceedings are complete and you have been allowed to remain in the country as a permanent resident.

◆ Terrorist acts
◆ Persecution of anyone because of race, religion, national origin, political opinion, or social group

Source: www.uscis.gov

☆ **FRAUD:** an act of deceiving or misrepresenting

If you are male, you are required to register with the Selective Service. In order to be eligible for naturalization, one of the following must be true:

◆ You are a female, OR
◆ You are a male registered with the Selective Service, OR
◆ You are a male who did not enter the United States under any status until after your 26th birthday, OR
◆ You are a male who was born before January 1, 1960, OR
◆ You are a male who was in the United States between the ages of 18 and 26 but who did not register with the Selective Service, and you will send a "Status Information Letter" from the Selective Service, explaining why you did not register, with your application.

☆ **SELECTIVE SERVICE:** a system under which men are called up for military service

If you are female, you do not need to worry about registering with the Selective Service. If you are male, however, you do. This applies only to men who entered the United States *under any status* before their 26th birthday. For some men, this requirement is more confusing than the physical presence requirement. *Status* can mean nonimmigrant visa classification, asylee, refugee, temporary protected, or parolee.

The background on this requirement is that U.S. federal law requires that all men who are at least 18, but not yet 26, register with the Selective Service. This applies to U.S. citizens, noncitizen immigrants, and undocumented aliens—all men living in the United States.

This requirement **does not** mean you are joining the U.S. military. Many immigrants may think this is the case, but it is not. Registering only means that you are telling the U.S. government *who you are* and *how to contact you* if there is a national emergency requiring men to be called to serve in the military. Keep in mind that even if there were a national emergency at some time in the future, not all men would be called to serve in the military.

Did You Know . . .

... if you are a member of the Armed Forces, you may be eligible for citizenship after only three years of permanent residence in the United States, two years faster than the customary five-year residency period. In addition, your application (the N-400 Military Naturalization Packet) is screened by the Armed Forces and forwarded directly to the USCIS, considerably speeding up the application process. For more information, contact your personnel officer or the USCIS.

If you entered the United States before you turned 26, you must register or you will not be eligible for naturalization. Furthermore, if you entered the United States before you turned 18, you must register within 30 days of your 18th birthday. If you failed to register within those 30 days, or if you have not yet turned 26 and have not registered, *do it now*. The Selective Service will accept late registrations only up to your 26th birthday, so it is critical for you to fulfill this requirement immediately. Even though late registration will be accepted, you are still in violation of the law if you do not register within 30 days of turning 18, or within 30 days of becoming a permanent resident if you are older than 18.

To register, pick up the forms at your local post office or visit the Selective Service website at www.sss.gov/regver/Register1.asp.

If you registered with the Selective Service, you must provide your Selective Service number on your application. If you have misplaced your Selective Service number, you can call 1-847-688-6888 to get your number.

If you are 26 or older and were required to register with the Selective Service but did not do so, you must contact Selective Service directly. You can call them at 1-847-688-6888 and you will be instructed to fill out a questionnaire and receive a "Status Information Letter."

> If a man does not register with the Selective Service as per federal law, he is barred from:
> - ➤ U.S. citizenship (if applying)
> - ➤ Government jobs
> - ➤ Federal student loans and grants for college or graduate study
> - ➤ JTPA (Job Training Partnership Act) Program vocational training

You must never have deserted from the U.S. Armed Forces.

If you left any branch of the U.S. Armed Forces before you were discharged, you deserted. This means you are not eligible for naturalization.

You must never have received an exemption or discharge from the U.S. Armed Forces on the grounds that you are an alien.

If you had to leave the U.S. Armed Forces because you are an alien, you are not eligible for naturalization.

You must be willing to perform either military OR civilian service for the United States if required by law.

If your religious teachings and beliefs prohibit you from performing military service, you must be willing to perform nonmilitary service. You will be required to send a letter explaining why your religious beliefs preclude you from fighting or serving in the military. Be concise and truthful in your explanation. In your letter, you should ask for a modified Oath of Allegiance to the United States.

☆ **PROHIBIT:** to prevent from doing something

If the USCIS accepts your request, you will take the Oath, omitting the words "to bear arms on behalf of the United States when required by law."

You must support the U.S. Constitution.

This is also called *attachment to the Constitution.* By supporting or attaching yourself to the U.S. Constitution, you are saying that you are willing to support the United States and the Constitution. You will declare your support when you recite

" . . . I will support and defend the Constitution and the laws of the United States of America against all enemies, foreign and domestic; that I will bear faith and allegiance to the same . . . "

in the Oath of Allegiance to the United States.

You must understand and be willing to take an Oath of Allegiance to the United States.

You are not a citizen until you take the Oath of Allegiance to the United States! It is a good idea to familiarize yourself with the Oath of Allegiance now. Get comfortable with the words and what they mean. If you feel that you cannot, in good conscience, take the oath, then you are not ready to become a U.S. citizen.

Did You Know . . .

. . . that the U.S. law allots 226,000 green cards each year in the family-based immigration category. Here's why: The USCIS processes immigration applications for immediate relatives faster than for non-immediate relatives. According to the USCIS, foreign nationals may be eligible to immigrate to the United States through a family member. Family members are classified as either *immediate relatives* or *non-immediate relatives*. Immediate relatives will be granted a green card soon after they apply, while non-immediate relatives must often wait years before getting a green card. Immediate relatives are: husband or wife of a U.S. citizen, an unmarried child (under 21) of a U.S. citizen, a parent of a U.S. citizen, and a U.S. citizen who is at least 21 years old.

Source: www.immigralaw.com

If you have read through this chapter and you have questions about whether or not you are eligible, use the resources listed in Appendices A and C. If you still question your eligibility, you may wish to consult with an immigration lawyer. One online legal resource is www.lawguru.com. They offer flat-fee legal advice and will answer some immigration and naturalization questions for free. Once you figure out your eligibility status, go to Chapter 3 for information on how to fill out the N-400 application to apply for citizenship.

☆ ☆ ☆
BRIGIT'S STORY

I HAVE been living in the United States for about 25 years. My family moved from England to the United States when I was eight years old. Adjusting from a small town in the English countryside to New York City was definitely a trying experience for a little girl. On my first day of school in the States it seemed like all the American kids were trying to imitate my British accent, and all I could think was, "You're the ones with funny accents!" Funny accents aside, being a native speaker of English definitely helped me to adjust to life in my new country. I enjoyed growing up in the United States, but I never contemplated becoming a citizen until the presidential elections in 1996. I was 25 and had made a life for myself in the United States, and the election would directly affect me, yet because I couldn't vote, I had no voice in the election. That's when I decided to become a citizen.

Getting started was the most difficult part of the citizenship application process. The first step I took was to call the USCIS hotline. I quickly discovered that it was very hard to get information over the phone. The website was much more helpful: I just typed my information into the fillable forms and printed them out. Then, I just had to wait until I received something in the mail about the next step. The best advice I can give anyone applying for citizenship is to be extremely patient, and don't be afraid to ask questions.

As for the test, mine was an oral interview with just ten questions, and there was no writing required. I studied hard for the interview, but the questions I was asked were pretty basic. I think it took about 11 months from filling out the very first form to getting sworn in. The swearing-in ceremony was really great. I was sworn in in Brooklyn along with about 400 others from all over the world. I was amazed to discover that they have three ceremonies a week, each with about the same number of new citizens. People were all dressed up with family members there to witness their naturalization. The judge gave a great speech about how the only pieces of paper he has on his office wall are his grandfather's naturalization papers and the letter appointing him as a judge. Even though I viewed the whole process as a bureaucratic hassle up to that point, I was really touched by the ceremony, and very glad to become a citizen of the United States.

CHAPTER 3

How to Apply for Citizenship

YOU HAVE DECIDED that you are ready to become a U.S. citizen and you have determined that you are fully eligible. The next step you need to take is to apply for citizenship.

To do this, you need a Form N-400: Application for Naturalization. You will need to contact the USCIS to get this form. You can contact your local USCIS office, call 1-800-375-5283, or visit the USCIS website at www.uscis.gov, to download the forms or even fill them out on the computer before printing them out.

Advantages of Naturalization

➤ The right to vote in federal, state, and local elections

➤ Freedom from deportation—U.S. citizens cannot be deported

➤ The ability to travel with a U.S. passport, thus reducing the need for applying for visas

➤ Greater employment opportunity—some jobs, including government jobs, require U.S. citizenship

Completing Form N-400

For 2002, the USCIS has published a completely new version of the N-400 form. All older versions are unacceptable; so make sure that you are using the current form. A sample form is included in Appendix C. It is a good idea to familiarize yourself with the form. You also may want to make a few copies of it and fill out a first draft. This will help you to be sure that you have all the information you need in order to answer all of the questions. The form that you hand in to the USCIS should be neat, easy to read, and free of errors and cross outs. The USCIS wesite has a form that can be filled out online and printed out under the "Forms and Fees" section at www.uscis.gov/graphics/formsfees/forms/N-400.htm.

Part 1. Your name:

This first part asks you about your name. Here, you should answer with your current legal name. If your name on your Permanent Resident Card is different from your legal name (even if it is misspelled on your card), make sure you document this in question B. You will also be asked to provide any other names you may have ever used. In addition, when you are being naturalized, you have the option to legally change your name. You can find out more about this option in the USCIS's *Guide to Naturalization.*

Part 2. Basis for eligibility:

Here, you will be asked to select the way in which you are eligible. Have you lived in the United States as a lawful permanent resident for at least five years? Have you lived in the United States as a lawful permanent resident for at least three years *and* been married to a U.S. citizen for those three years? Do you have qualifying military service?

Check only one box in Part 2.

Part 3. Information about you:

This part asks for basic information—the date you became a permanent resident, date of birth, country of birth, Social Security number, and your alien registration number (A-number) found on your alien registration card. Are you married? Are you the child of U.S. citizens? Also, if you are requesting accommodations and/or waivers of certain requirements based on disability or impairment, this part is where you would state that information. Be sure to answer these questions honestly!

Part 4. Addresses and telephone numbers:

This part asks you for your home and mailing addresses (if they are different from each other), as well as gives you the option to provide your telephone number and e-mail addresses.

☆ **A-NUMBER:** your alien registration number

Part 5. Information for criminal records search:

The information asked for in this part is used, in conjunction with your fingerprints, by the Federal Bureau of Investigation (FBI) to search for criminal records.

Part 6. Information about your residence and employment:

Complete this part with details about your residence and employment for the past five years. Be specific and honest. Remember to list jobs and addresses in reverse chronological order, starting with the most recent.

Part 7. Time outside the United States:

You will need to know specific details regarding your travel history to answer the questions in this part. This means that you must provide information about all trips outside the United States (even if only for a day) for the preceding five (or three) year period, as of the date of your application. Attach additional sheets of paper, if necessary. If there were any trips that lasted longer than six months, be prepared to explain why.

Part 8. Information about your marital history:

If you are married, you will need to provide information about your spouse including his or her name, address, date of birth, country of birth, citizenship, and Social Security number. You also need to provide your spouse's A-number, immigration status, and information about naturalization, if these are applicable.

If you or your spouse has been married previously, you will need to provide information on those marriages.

Part 9. Information about your children:

This part requires information regarding the total number of children you have, if any. If you have children, you will provide their full names, dates and countries of birth, citizenship, A-numbers, and addresses.

Part 10. Additional questions:

This part asks 39 questions designed to determine what additional eligibility factors apply to you, if any. These are in addition to those listed in Part 2. Check *yes* or *no* to answer each question. You will be asked to list any and all organizations, funds, groups, clubs, etc., to which you belong or have belonged in the past. If you have never belonged to any clubs, check *no* in the space provided. In Part 10, you will also find a section with six questions called *Oath Requirements* that questions the level of your commitment to the United States. If you answer *no* to any of the questions, you will have to supply an explanation for your answer on a separate sheet. Again, it is important that you answer each question honestly.

Providing honest answers is essential to the process. The bottom line is to understand what you are being asked and to answer the questions accurately. It is advisable to provide explanations to any questions regarding circumstances and final results of arrest and any supporting documents.

Part 11. Signature:

Make sure you sign your application! Your application will not be accepted if it is not signed.

Part 12. Signature of person preparing form, if other than above:

If you have someone prepare your form for you, this person will have to sign your application form as well.

Part 13. Signature at interview:

This part requires you and your interviewer to sign at the time and place of your interview. *Do not* complete this section until you are instructed to do so by the person interviewing you.

Part 14. Oath of Allegiance:

By signing this final part, you acknowledge your willingness to take the Oath of Allegiance if your application is accepted. As with Part 13, *do not* complete this section until you are instructed to do so by the person interviewing you.

After you have filled out your form, review it and make sure you have completed all of the questions honestly and completely. Put your name and A-number on any additional sheets that you have attached to your application.

Note: It is critical that you answer *all* questions. If you do not, the USCIS may have to send your application back to you so you can complete it. This can considerably delay your application.

Your Cover Letter

Your cover letter should list the information included in your application. If you are sending only a Form N-400, you should write that. If you are sending additional forms, list them. This is also your opportunity to request that your interview/test be given at the same time and place as another applicant, if you wish. Be sure to include that applicant's name and A-number.

On the next page is a sample cover letter to help you create your own letter.

Antonio A. Gianninni
314 West 178 Street, #4R
New York, NY 10024
212-555-5434
Alien Registration #A0123456789

November 17, 2005

USCIS Vermont Service Center
Att: N-400 Unit
75 Lower Welden Street
Saint Albans, VT 05479-0001

To Whom It May Concern:

Please accept my enclosed and complete Application
for Naturalization. Included with my application you
will find 1) a photocopy of my Alien Registration
Card, 2) three color photographs as per your
specifications, 3) a photocopy of my passport, and 4)
a check for $400 U.S. dollars for the application and
fingerprinting fees, payable to USCIS.

If possible, I would like to request that my interview
be scheduled at the same time and place as my wife,
Alba Gianninni, Alien Registration #A0987654321.

I thank you for your time and consideration.

Sincerely,

Antonio Antonello Gianninni

Antonio Antonello Gianninni

Enclosures.

Payment

Please double-check with your service center, as some may prefer checks to be made out to the U.S. Treasury. Your payment will consist of a $330 filing fee and a $70 fingerprinting fee. These fees can be combined in one payment of $400. (Check with the USCIS before sending money to make sure this fee hasn't increased since the publication of this book.) You will make a check or money order payable to the U.S. Citizenship and Immigration Services. The USCIS *does not* accept cash. Be sure that you send only a check or a money order. Whether you send a check or a money order, your payment must be drawn on a bank or institution located in the United States and must be payable in U.S. dollars.

There are two exceptions to the above. If you live in Guam, you should make your check or money order payable to "Treasurer, Guam." If you live in the U.S. Virgin Islands, you should make your check or money order payable to "Commissioner of Finance of the Virgin Islands."

Photographs

You are required to submit three photographs of yourself along with your application. Starting August 2, 2004, the USCIS announced a change in photo requirements from a $\frac{3}{4}$ frontal view to a standard, full-frontal view used in passport photos. These should be color photos taken within 30 days of submitting your application. The photos should measure $2'' \times 2''$. You can get your pictures taken at any place where passport photos are done, such as the post office. Check the yellow pages in your local phone book.

Specifically, USCIS requires that your photos:

◆ Are identical
◆ Are glossy, unretouched, and unmounted
◆ Have a white background
◆ Show a face dimension of about 1 inch from chin to top of hair
◆ Show a full-frontal view of your face.

You should write your name and A-number on the back of each photo. Try to do so lightly so that your writing pressure does not damage the front of the photo. Refer to the informational flyer in Appendix C for more details.

Permanent Resident Card (Alien Registration Receipt Card or "Green Card")

Make a photocopy of the front and back of your card. This copy should be clear enough so that anyone looking at it can easily read all information. Also, photocopy your passport information.

Red Tape

Often, government agencies have very formal procedures that don't seem to have an immediately clear reason for existence. In the United States, we call this form of bureaucracy *red tape*. Having to handle red tape can lead to frustration. When you find yourself losing your temper because of red tape, imagine yourself tangled up in miles of red masking tape. This should make you laugh or smile, defusing your anger.

☆ **BUREAUCRACY:** a system of administration marked by strict adherence to many rules

Assembling Your Application

Before you assemble your application and mail it, use this checklist to ensure you have all of the required elements:

Application Checklist

_____ Cover letter

_____ Complete Form N-400

_____ One check for $400 payable to the U.S. Citzenship and Immigration Services to cover the filing fee of $330 and fingerprint fee of $70

_____ Three color photographs, 2" × 2"

_____ Copy of the front and back of your Permanent Resident Card (green card)

_____ Supporting documents, such as income tax returns

_____ Envelope addressed to the USCIS Service Center with jurisdiction over your state

Once your application is complete, you should make a photocopy of every page. Keep your copies in a safe place. It is recommended that you use the return receipt option at the post office or a delivery confirmation from an express carrier.

Where to Send Your Application

There are four USCIS Service Centers that accept Form N-400. Where you will send your application depends upon where you currently live. Use the following list to determine where to send your application.

If you live in:
Alabama
Arkansas
Florida
Georgia
Kentucky
Louisiana
Mississippi
New Mexico
North Carolina
South Carolina
Oklahoma
Tennessee
Texas

You will send your application to:
USCIS Texas Service Center
Attention N-400 Unit
P.O. Box 851204
Mesquite, TX 75185-1204

If you live in:
　Connecticut
　Delaware
　District of Columbia (Washington, D.C.)
　Maine
　Maryland
　Massachusetts
　New Hampshire
　New Jersey
　New York
　Pennsylvania
　Puerto Rico
　Rhode Island
　Vermont
　U.S. Virgin Islands
　Virginia
　West Virginia

You will send your application to:
USCIS Vermont Service Center
Attention N-400 Unit
75 Lower Welden Street
St. Albans, VT 05479-0001

If you live in:
　Arizona
　California
　Guam
　Hawaii
　Nevada

You will send your application to:
USCIS California Service Center
Attention N-400 Unit
P.O. Box 10400
Laguna Niguel, CA 92607-1040

If you live in:
  Alaska
  Colorado
  Idaho
  Illinois
  Indiana
  Iowa
  Kansas
  Michigan
  Minnesota
  Missouri
  Montana
  Nebraska
  North Dakota
  Ohio
  Oregon
  South Dakota
  Utah
  Washington
  Wisconsin
  Wyoming

You will send your application to:
USCIS Nebraska Service Center
Attention N-400 Unit
P.O. Box 87400
Lincoln, NE 68501-7400

After You Have Submitted Your Application

The first thing that will happen after you submit your application is that you will receive a letter from the USCIS telling you when and where to go to be fingerprinted. You should make every attempt to go to this appointment and not reschedule. At every step in this process, rescheduling causes *long delays*. Bring your appointment letter with you when you go to be fingerprinted. Also, you also should bring your Permanent Residence Card and another photo ID. We will discuss fingerprinting again in the next chapter.

Changing Your Address

It is important that you notify the USCIS every time you change your address after you have submitted your application. If you don't, USCIS correspondence—such as your interview appointment notification—will be sent to your old address. This could set your application back months, or even years. It is recommended that applicants try not to move until the interview takes place. It sometimes takes months for a change of address form to get associated with your file.

The USCIS will inform you of your interview/oral exam date in an official letter. Usually, the interview will be scheduled for six to nine months after your application was submitted. Keep this letter with the copies of your application. Remember, it is critical that you keep all of this information in a safe place.

The next chapter will introduce you to some of the types of questions you will be expected to answer during your interview. Use this information as a starting place for your interview/oral exam preparation.

Tips for Assembling Your Application

_____ Print clearly with black ink or, better yet, type your answers. It is recommended that you use the fillable Adobe Acrobat version on the website.

_____ Check your application for spelling errors.

_____ Double-check your application to be sure that you have completed all items on the form.

_____ Before inserting your application into the mailing envelope, make copies of every page. Keep these copies in a safe place for future reference.

_____ Make your check payable to the U.S. Citizenship and Immigration Services—do not send cash.

_____ Clearly mark both the envelope and your cover letter with the form type: N-400 Application for Naturalization.

_____ Use the correct mailing address.

_____ Gather all supporting documents and include copies.

When you go to your USCIS interview, you will be asked many questions based on the answers you submit on your N-400. Sometimes, answers will change from the time you filled out the N-400 form until the time that you have your interview. Be prepared to explain any discrepancies, and remember to make a copy of your N-400 form so that you can review it prior to your interview. In addition, provide a list of any excursions outside of the United States since the filing the N-400. Remember, you are still subject to the Physical Presence and Continuous Residency requirement until the time of your naturalization interview.

☆ **DISCREPANCY:** divergence or disagreement, as between facts or claims; difference

Checklist

Documents you may need to include with your N-400:

All applicants must send:

_____ A photocopy of both sides of your Permanent Resident Card (previously known as Alien Registration Card);

_____ Three color photographs (full-frontal face position); AND

_____ A check or money order for $400

If an attorney or accredited representative is acting on your behalf, send:

_____ Form G-28, "Notice of Entry of Appearance as Attorney or Representative"

If your current name is different than the name on your Permanent Resident Card, send:

_____ The document that legally changed your name (marriage license, divorce decree, OR court document) OR a detailed explanation of why you use a different name

If you are applying for naturalization on the basis of marriage to a U.S. citizen, send:

_____ Proof that your spouse has been a U.S. citizen for at least the past three years (birth certificate, naturalization certificate, certificate of citizenship, copy of the inside of the front cover, and signature part of your spouse's valid U.S. passport, OR Form FS-240, "Consular Report of Birth Abroad of a Citizen of the United States of America");

_____ Your current marriage certificate;

_____ Proof of termination of ALL of yours and your spouse's prior marriages (divorce decree OR death certificate); AND

_____ An original IRS Form 1722 listing tax information for the past three years OR copies of the income tax form you filed for the past three years.

☆ **DECREE:** an order usually having the force of law

If you have ever been in the U.S. military, send:

_____ An original Form N-426, "Request for Certification of Military or Naval Service"; AND

_____ An original Form G-325B, "Biographic Information."

If you have taken a trip outside the United States that lasted for six months or more since becoming a permanent resident, send:

_____ An original IRS Form 1722 listing tax information for the past five years (or for the past three years if you are applying on the basis of marriage to a U.S. citizen) OR copies of income tax returns filed in the last three years.

If you have a dependent spouse or children, and have been ordered to provide financial support, send:

_____ Copies of the court or government order to provide financial support; AND

_____ Evidence that you have complied with the court or government order (cancelled checks, money order receipts, a court or agency printout of child support payments, OR evidence of wage garnishments).

If you have ever been arrested or detained by any law enforcement officer for any reason and NO charges were filed, send:

_____ An official statement from the arresting agency or applicable court indicating that no charges were filed. It is recommended that individuals with any criminal issues consult an attorney (not a paralegal/notary). Serious consequences, such as possible initiation of deportation proceedings may occur.

If you have ever been arrested or detained by any law enforcement officer for any reason and charges were filed, send:

_____ An original or certified copy of the complete court disposition for each incident (dismissal order, conviction record, OR acquittal order).

If you have ever been convicted or placed in an alternative sentencing program or rehabilitative program, send:

_____ The sentencing record for each incident; AND
_____ Evidence that you completed your sentence (probation record, parole record, OR evidence that you completed an alternative sentencing program or rehabilitative program).

If you have ever had any arrest or conviction vacated, set aside, sealed, expunged, or otherwise removed from your record, send:

_____ An original or certified copy of the court order vacating, settling aside, sealing, expunging, or otherwise removing the arrest or conviction.

☆ **EXPUNGED:** to be erased or struck out

If you have ever failed to file an income tax return when it was required by law, send:

_____ Copies of all correspondence with the Internal Revenue Service (IRS) regarding your failure to file.

If you have any federal, state, or local taxes that are overdue, send:

_____ A signed agreement from the IRS, state, or local tax office showing that you have filed a tax return and arranged to pay the taxes you owe; AND

_____ Documentation from the IRS, state, or local tax office showing the current status of your repayment program.

If you are applying for a disability exception to the testing requirement, send:

_____ An original Form N-648, "Medical Certification for Disability Exceptions," completed by a licensed medical doctor or licensed clinical psychologist. (A list of USCIS-approved physicians may be obtained from the USCIS office or website.)

If you did not register with the Selective Service and you 1) are male, 2) are 26 years of age or older, and 3) lived in the United States other than as a lawful nonimmigrant between the ages of 18 and 26, send:

_____ A "Status Information Letter" from the Selective Service (call 1-847-688-6888 for more information).

Source: U.S. Citizenship and Immigration Services, *A Guide to Naturalization,* U.S. Government Printing Office: Washington, D.C., 2004

If you know for sure that you are prepared to accept all the responsibilities that becoming a citizen of the United States entails, then you are ready to start on your path to citizenship. Remember, before you can apply for naturalization, you must first determine if you're eligible. Once you are sure that you are eligible, your next step is obtaining and filling out the USCIS's Form N-400. Before you set out to fill out this form, gather any and all information about yourself that you have collected since you arrived in the United States. This includes all marriage certificates, birth certificates of your children (if you have any), all documents you may have received from the government, and so forth. Know your A-number, and know the A-numbers of your spouse and your children if they have any. If you are a male under the age of 26, make sure you are registered with the Selective Service. If you are not registered, YOU ARE NOT ELIGIBLE, and you won't be until you register. Most importantly, *be honest* when answering these questions. And don't rush through them. If you read through the directions carefully, and take your time answering each question thoughtfully, you'll be fine. Good luck!

☆ ☆ ☆
RAVI'S STORY

I MADE the decision to leave India and come to the United States when I was 25 years old. It was quite a scary proposition, because I would be leaving my friends and family behind and going to a huge country where I did not know a soul. My mother and father were worried about me going alone, but growing up I had heard stories of men who moved from India to America and became extremely successful and prosperous—I was determined to do the same; and when I did I would send for my parents. I learned to speak English as a child, and it was a small comfort for me to know that at least I would be able to communicate when I arrived in New York.

It was very hard at first, but I quickly discovered that there was a large Indian community in New York, and I met many people from all over the world who had come to America with the same dream as me, and most were more than happy to help me out as others had done for them when they first arrived. My first few years here were spent working at any job I could find at night, and then going to school during the day. There were some days I thought I would never make it, but eventually my hard work paid off and now I am a pharmacist, have a family of my own, and was finally able to afford to send for my parents. They were very proud. I will never forget the look on my father's face when he came here. It was worth all the years of hardship.

I was living in the United States for quite a while before I decided to become a citizen. Twenty-seven years had passed, and America had truly become my home country—I wanted to be able to vote, travel as an American without worrying about obtaining visas, and when the time comes, to be able to properly plan my estate. I spoke to a few friends who had already gone through the process, and they told me to go to an USCIS office. The hardest part was filling out the paperwork and waiting in the lines. At first, I was afraid of doing poorly on the history portion of the interview, so I decided to study using a citizenship book and some previous questionnaires from friends who were already citizens. In the end, understanding the U.S. Constitution and learning American history became one of my favorite parts of the whole process. But nothing beat the feeling of seeing the other happy faces during the swearing-in ceremony. It was at that moment that I truly realized I had fulfilled my dream. The most important piece of advice I can offer to someone who wants to become a U.S. citizen is to get going soon and do it. It is important and it is worthwhile.

CHAPTER 4

The USCIS Interview and Oral Exam/Sample Questions and Answers

AFTER YOU HAVE completed the naturalization process, you must wait for notification from the USCIS regarding your next step.

> ☆ **NOTIFICATION:** something, such as a letter, by which notice is given

After the N-400 Is Filed

Typically, it can take a few months to hear from the USCIS. If you haven't heard from the USCIS in writing for over 90 days, it is a good idea to call the USCIS toll-free number, 1-800-375-5283, for assistance and to ensure that they have received your N-400 application.

In many cases, it's normal for the USCIS to call or write to you for more information on your case if the answers you provided are unclear or confusing in some way. Sometimes, the USCIS will return your N-400 application if information is missing or incomplete. Again, it is very important to fill out the N-400 completely and accurately. If the USCIS contacts you, respond within the allotted time. If you don't, your application may be considered abandoned.

When the USCIS does contact you, remember to refer to the copy of the filled-out N-400 that you kept for your records. This will help make the procedure run smoothly for you. If your N-400 is in order, the USCIS will contact you in approximately 90 to 120 days. They will send you written notification to appear at the USCIS office in your area for fingerprinting. Remember to also keep your application receipt number, which will allow you to check your case status online at https://egov.immigration.gov/cris/jsps/index.jsp.

Fingerprinting

You should try very hard to make the fingerprinting appointment at your allotted time. Sometimes, the USCIS office has a make-up day on which candidates can show up for fingerprinting. You could wait around for a long time if you live in an urban area, so this is to be avoided.

Your fingerprints are then forwarded to the FBI for clearance, along with your file. The FBI will conduct a complete background check for a criminal past both within the United States and abroad to ensure that you do not have any warrants out for arrest and to verify further the information you provided on the N-400. Getting clearance from the FBI can take 60 to 90 days, so be patient. Once you have clearance from the FBI, your USCIS interview will be scheduled.

After FBI clearance, you will receive a written notification of your USCIS interview date and time. The date of the interview can be anywhere from one to two and a half years from the date you receive it. You should do everything you can to make sure that you will be able to appear on this date. Attempting to change the assigned date could lead to major delays in your process.

Did You Know . . .

. . . that between 1990 and 2000, the Asian population in the United States grew by 72%, to nearly 12 million people.

Source: US. Census 2000.

The USCIS Interview

Keep in mind that the USCIS interview is not just to test your knowledge of U.S. history and government. The USCIS examiner is charged with:

◆ Verifying the accuracy of your N-400 application
◆ Ensuring that you have good moral character
◆ Making sure that you can read, write, understand, and speak English

However, if you are exempt from the language portion for a legitimate reason, it will be noted in your file, and the USCIS examiner will not test you in those areas.

What to Bring to Your Interview

While it is natural to be nervous, remember that if you have studied and prepared thoroughly for your interview, you should have nothing to worry about. One way to ensure that you are prepared is to gather ahead of time all of the items you'll need to bring to your interview. You should bring *all* of the following documents—both originals and copies for all the USCIS to keep with your records. These should be original or certified copies and in *English*. If your documents are not in English, a certified translator must translate them and they must be marked as such. Translators cannot be an interested party, friend, or family member.

➤ Photo identification
➤ Permanent Resident Card
➤ Passport
➤ Any travel documents issued by the USCIS
➤ Copies of your tax returns from the past five years
➤ Selective Service registration card (if you are male)

➤ Any arrest reports, certified court dispositions, or probation reports that you might have

➤ If you have arranged to take an alternate Oath of Allegiance for religious reasons, you should bring supporting documents (such as a letter from your religious organization)

➤ Proof of support of all minor children residing outside of your home (cancelled checks, money orders, court documents)

As you proceed with the interview, some information, such as a job, or address, or even an area code may have changed since you filed the N-400. This is perfectly normal. The USCIS officer will simply make the change in your file and continue with the interview. There is no reason to lie about a change in job or address—it will not put your application at risk.

Remember, as you answer the questions about your N-400 application, the examiner is not just verifying your information; he or she is also assessing your ability to listen and understand English, as well as your ability to speak correctly in English.

Next, the USCIS examiner tests you on a selection from the official U.S. history and civics questions. (The complete list of official USCIS questions and answers appears in Chapter 6.)

Making a Study Plan

To pass the citizenship oral interview, you need a study plan that will help you prepare. Follow these directions.

Step 1: Set a time frame

You should allow anywhere from *six to 12 months* to prepare for the citizenship test.

Step 2: Get the correct information

Check filing dates for the test. Double-check your information. Read the directions and suggestions for success that come with the papers you receive from the USCIS.

Step 3: Get all your materials

Find some review books or other materials you might need to prepare for the test. Try *Pass the U.S. Citizenship Exam.* If you have access to the Internet, you can find information online. Find out if there are any citizenship preparation courses available to you in your community.

Step 4: Make a study schedule

Below, you will see a study schedule chart. Fill it out, and stick to your plan.

Step 5: Stick to your plan and reward yourself for it

Treat yourself to an afternoon walk, a candy bar, a long phone chat with a friend—anything that will reward you for maintaining a good study schedule. It isn't easy and you should pat yourself on the back when you can stick to your routine for some period of time.

Create a Study Plan Schedule

When you find out when your appointment is, answer the following questions. When you're finished, you will have a study schedule.

The test I need to take is _____.

It will be held on _____.

It will be given at this time _____.

The test site is located at _____.

Three questions I have about the test are:

_____

_____

_____

I plan to study for this test as follows:

Six months before the test: _____

_____

Five months before the test: _____

_____

Four months before the test: _____

_____

Three months before the test: _____

_____

Two months before the test: _____

_____

One month before the test: _____

_____

Two weeks before the test: _____

_____

One week before the test: _____

_____

Two days before the test: _____

_____

The day before the test: _____

_____

Greetings and Small Talk

At the USCIS testing facility, the interviewer will call your name and lead you to an office. Before starting the actual interview, he or she will begin with some general conversation, or small talk, to see how good your English is. If the interviewer feels that he or she cannot successfully communicate with you in English, the interview may be ended. Here are some questions that the interviewer might ask you.

"How Are You?" Questions

Q: How are you?

A: I am <u>fine</u> / <u>good</u> / <u>great</u>. OR <u>Fine</u> / <u>Good, thank you</u>.

Q: How is the weather today?

A: The weather is <u>fine</u> / <u>good</u> / <u>cold</u> / <u>warm</u> / <u>sunny</u> / <u>rainy</u> / <u>windy</u>. (Pick which one applies.)

Q: How did you get here today?

A: I came by <u>car</u> / <u>bus</u> / <u>subway</u> / <u>train</u>. OR My <u>son</u> / <u>daughter</u> brought me.

Why You Are Here

Q: Do you understand why you are here today?

A: <u>Yes.</u>

Q: Why are you here today?

A: <u>For my citizenship interview.</u> OR <u>Because I want to be a U.S. citizen.</u>

Q: Why do you want to become a U.S. citizen?

A: <u>Because I love America.</u> (Use your own reason!)

Beginning the Interview

Q: Do you have any questions before we begin?

A: <u>No.</u>

Preparation and Study

Q: Have you prepared for the citizenship test?

A: <u>**Yes.**</u>

Q: Have you studied for the citizenship test?

A: <u>**Yes.**</u>

Q: How did you study / prepare?

A: <u>I read a book.</u> OR <u>I took a class.</u> OR <u>My children helped me.</u>

Truth Oath and Identity Check

Now the interviewer will ask you to take the truth oath. He or she will ask you to swear that you will tell the truth during the interview. Here is what you may hear. Say these phrases out loud several times.

Interviewer: "Okay, let's begin. Please stand and raise your right hand."
What you do: Get out of your chair and put your right hand in the air.
What it means: You are getting ready to take an oath, or promise.

Interviewer: "Do you promise to tell the truth and nothing but the truth so help you God?" OR "Do you swear that everything you say today will be the truth?"
What you do: Answer out loud, "<u>Yes.</u>"
What it means: You promise to tell the truth. You promise to tell no lies.

Interviewer: "Please sit down." OR "You can sit down now."
What you do: Sit down in your chair again.
What it means: The oath is finished.

Extra Practice

Q: Do you understand what an oath is?
A: <u>**Yes, it is a promise to tell the truth.**</u>

The interviewer will then check your identity, and you will have to show your verification information, such as the Appointment Notice and Alien Registration Card.

Interviewer: "At this point, I have to check your identity. I need to see your **Appointment Notice** or **Invitation to Appear**. I would also like to see your passport if you have one, and your **Alien Registration Card**.
What you do: Show the letter you received in the mail from USCIS, which is called your **Appointment Notice** or **Invitation to Appear**. Then, show your **Alien Registration Card**.
What it means: You can prove who you are.

After the interviewer has checked your identity, the actual interview will begin.

Typical N-400 Questions and Answers

Your interviewer will go through your N-400 form to check the information you wrote. Be sure to keep a copy of your N-400 form to review the answers to all the following questions.

N-400 Parts 1 & 2: Your Name and Information about Your Eligibility

Q: What is your name?

A: My name is _____.

Q: Spell your last name.

A: __-__-__-__-__-__-__-__-__-__-__-__-__

Q: When did you first come to the United States?

A: I came to the United States on _____ (month, day, year).

Q: How long have you been a permanent resident?

A: _____ years

Q: Have you ever used a different name?

A: <u>Yes</u> / <u>No</u>

Q: Do you want to change your name?

A: <u>Yes</u> / <u>No</u> (If yes, say what you want to change it to.)

Q: To what do you want to change your name? OR
          What name do you want to have now?

A: _____

Q: What other names have you gone by? OR
          What other names have you used in the past?

A: _____ OR <u>None.</u>

Q: What was your maiden name?

A: Before I was married, my name was _____.

N-400 Part 3: Information about You

Q: How long have you been a permanent resident of the United States? OR

How long have you lived in the United States?

A: _____ years

Q: When did you become a permanent resident? OR

When did you first come to the United States? OR

On what date did you enter the United States?

A: _____ (month, day, year)

Q: You've been a permanent resident since _____, is that correct?

A: <u>Yes.</u> (If no, say the correct date.)

Q: Where did you enter the United States? OR

What was your port of entry? OR

In what port of entry did you arrive in America?

A: _____.

Q: What is your date of birth? OR

What is your birthday? OR

When were you born?

A: I was born on _____ (month, day, year).

Q: What is your country of birth? OR

Where were you born?

A: I was born in _____ (country).

Q: What is your nationality? OR

What is your current citizenship?

A: I am _____ (nationality).

Q: What is your Social Security number?

(**NOTE:** You might NOT want to write your Social Security number in this book, but it is a very good idea to memorize it.)

A: My Social Security number is __ __ __ - __ __ - __ __ __ __.

Q: What is your marital status?
A: I am <u>single</u> / <u>married</u> / <u>divorced</u> / <u>widowed</u>.

Q: Are you married?
A: <u>Yes</u> / <u>No</u>

Q: Have you ever been divorced?
A: <u>Yes</u> / <u>No</u>

Q: How long have you been married?
A: I have been married for _____ years.

N-400 Part 4: Addresses and Telephone Numbers

Q: What is your home address? OR
          Where do you live?
A: I live at _____.

Q: What is your home phone number? OR
          What is your telephone number at home?
A: My phone number is __ __ __-__ __ __-__ __ __ __.

Q: Do you have a work telephone number?
A: <u>Yes</u> / <u>No</u> OR <u>No, I am not currently working.</u>

Q: What is your work phone number?
A: My work phone number is __ __ __-__ __ __-__ __ __ __.

N-400 Part 5: Information for Criminal Records Search

Q: What is your height? OR
          How tall are you?
A: I am _____ feet, _____ inches tall.

Q: What is your weight? OR
          How much do you weigh?
A: I weigh _____ pounds.

Q: What is your race?

A: I am <u>White</u> / <u>Asian</u> / <u>Black or African American</u> / <u>American Indian or Alaskan Native</u> / <u>Native Hawaiian or Other Pacific Islander</u> / <u>Other</u>: _____.

Q: What is your hair color? OR
What color is your hair?

A: My hair is <u>black</u> / <u>brown</u> / <u>blonde</u> / <u>gray</u> / <u>white</u> / <u>red</u> / <u>sandy</u> / <u>other</u>: _____. OR
<u>I am bald.</u>

Q: What is your eye color?

A: My eyes are <u>brown</u> / <u>blue</u> / <u>green</u> / <u>hazel</u> / <u>gray</u> / <u>black</u> / <u>other</u>: _____.

Your interviewer may ask you to answer the following questions with detailed information. Or, your interviewer may also just read off your N-400 form and ask you if that information is right. Be sure to know all the information on your N-400 form thoroughly. If your information changes after you mail in your N-400 form, be ready to explain the changes.

N-400 Part 6: Information about Your Residence and Employment

Q: Where have you lived in the past five years?

A: I have lived at _____ (list all addresses beginning with your current address).

Q: Are these all the places you have lived in the last five years?

A: <u>Yes</u> / <u>No</u> (If yes, explain why you did not write it on the form.)

Q: Have you lived in any other places in the last five years?

A: <u>Yes</u> / <u>No</u> (If yes, explain why you did not write it on the form.)

Q: Have you worked in the last five years?

A: <u>Yes</u> / <u>No</u>

Q: Are you currently employed? OR
Do you have a job?

A: Yes / No

Q: Why aren't you working?

A: (Be honest!)

Q: What is your occupation? OR
What do you do? OR
What kind of work do you do?

A: I am / was a _____. OR I am retired.

Q: Where do you work? OR
Who do you work for? OR
Who is your employer? OR
How do you support yourself?

A: I work at _____.

Q: How long have you worked there? OR
How long have you held this job?

A: I have worked there for _____ years.

Q: Who was your employer before that?

A: _____.

Q: Please list your employers of the past five years.

A: I have worked for _____ (list all employers).

Q: Is this list of employers complete?

A: Yes / No (If yes, explain why you did not write all your employers from the past five years on the form.)

N-400 Part 7: Time outside the United States

Q: Since becoming a permanent resident, have you ever left the United States? OR
Have you left the United States since you became a permanent resident? OR

Since coming to the United States, have you traveled to any other country? OR
Have you visited any other country since becoming a permanent resident?

A: <u>Yes</u> / <u>No</u>

Q: How many times have you left the United States since you became a permanent resident?

A: _____ times

Q: How long were you away?

A: I was gone for _____ <u>days</u> / <u>weeks</u> / <u>months</u> / <u>years</u>.

Q: Which country did you travel to? OR

Q: Where did you go?

A: I went to _____.

Q: Why did you leave the United States?

A: I left because _____.

Q: Did any of these trips last six months or more?

A: <u>Yes</u> / <u>No</u> (If yes, be prepared to explain why.)

Q: When was your most recent trip? OR

Q: When was the last time you left the United States?

A: It was _____.

Q: For how long were you in _____ (country)?

A: I was there for _____ <u>days</u> / <u>weeks</u> / <u>months</u> / <u>years</u>.

N-400 Part 8: Information about Your Marital History

The following questions ask about your marital status. If you have never been married, you do not need to review this section. Skip to Part 9 on page 54.

Q: What is your marital status?

A: I am <u>single</u> / <u>married</u> / <u>divorced</u> / <u>widowed</u>.

Q: Have you ever been married?

A: <u>Yes</u> / <u>No</u>

Q: Are you married?
A: <u>Yes</u> / <u>No</u>

Q: How many times have you been married?
A: I have been married ____ times.

Q: What is the full name of your husband / wife?
A: My husband's / wife's name is _____.

Q: What is your husband's / wife's date of birth?
A: __ __ / __ __ / __ __ __ __

Q: When did you marry him / her?
A: __ __ / __ __ / __ __ __ __

Q: What is his / her current address?
A: _____.

Q: Is your wife / husband a U.S. citizen?
A: <u>Yes</u> / <u>No</u>

Q: What is his / her immigration status?
A: <u>He</u> / <u>she is a permanent resident.</u> OR

A: <u>He</u> / <u>she is a U.S. citizen.</u>

Q: What is his / her country of citizenship?
A: _____.

Q: When did he / she become a U.S. citizen?
A: __ __ / __ __ / __ __ __ __.

Q: If your husband / wife is NOT a U.S. citizen, what is his / her country of origin?
A: <u>He</u> / <u>she is from</u> _____.

Q: If your husband / wife is NOT a U.S. citizen, what is his / her USCIS "A" number?
A: <u>His</u> / <u>her USCIS A number is</u> _____.

Q: Have you ever been divorced?
A: <u>Yes</u> / <u>No</u>

Q: Why did you get a divorce?

A: _____.

N-400 Part 9: Information about Your Children

Q: How many children do you have? OR
      How many sons and daughters do you have?

A: _____

Q: What are the full names of your sons and daughters?

A: (Say each child's first, middle, and last name.)

Q: Do your children live with you?

A: <u>Yes</u> / <u>No</u>

Q: How many people live in your house?

A: _____ people: myself, my husband / wife, and ___ children.

Q: Who do you live with?

A: I live with _____.

Q: Where do your children live?

A: My children live with me in _____. OR other:
      _____.

Q: Did any of your children stay in your native country?

A: <u>Yes</u> / <u>No</u>

Q: When were your children born?

A: One was born in _____, one in _____,
      and one in _____ (or more).

Q: Were they all born in the United States?

A: <u>Yes</u> / <u>No</u>

Additional Questions

The following questions are all yes or no questions. Pay attention to the beginning of each question, because that will give you a clue about how to answer it. However, make sure you know what each question is asking.

SENTENCE PATTERNS

For questions beginning with:	Answer:
"Have you ever . . ."	No
"Did you ever . . ."	No
"Do you owe . . ."	No
"Do you believe . . ."	Yes
"Do you support . . ."	Yes
"If the law requires it, are you willing . . ."	Yes

General Questions

Q: **Have you ever** claimed (in writing or in any other way) to be a U.S. citizen? OR

Have you ever pretended to be a U.S. citizen?

Q: **Have you ever** registered to vote in any federal, state, or local election in the United States? OR

Have you ever voted in any federal, state, or local election in the United States?

Q: Since becoming a lawful permanent resident, **have you ever** failed to file a required federal, state, or local tax return? OR

Do you owe any federal, state, or local taxes that are overdue?

Q: Do you have any title of nobility in any foreign country? OR

Were you born with or have you acquired any title of nobility? OR

Are you a king, queen, duke, earl, prince, or princess, or do you have any other title of nobility?

Q: **Have you ever** been declared legally incompetent or been confined to a mental institution within the last five years? OR **Have you ever** been in a mental hospital? OR **Have you ever** been confined as a patient in a mental institution?

A: No. (If yes, explain.)

Affiliations

Q: **Have you ever** been affiliated with any organization, association, fund, foundation, party, club, or society?

Q: **Have you ever** been a member of the Communist Party?

Q: **Have you ever** been a member of any other totalitarian party?

Q: **Have you ever** been a member of a terrorist organization?

Q: **Have you ever** advocated the overthrow of any government by force or violence?

Q: **Have you ever** persecuted any person because of race, religion, national origin, membership in a particular social group, or political opinion?

Q: **Have you ever** worked for or been associated with the Nazi government of Germany?

A: No. (If yes, explain why.)

Continuous Residence

Q: **Have you ever** called yourself a "nonresident" on a federal, state, or local tax return?

Q: **Have you ever** failed to file a federal, state, or local tax return because you considered yourself to be a nonresident?

A: No.

Paying Taxes

Q: **Have you ever** failed to file a federal income tax return?

Q: **Was there ever** a year when you didn't file your federal tax forms?

A: <u>No.</u> (If you have failed to file taxes, say "yes" and explain why.)

Q: Have you filed your federal taxes every year?

Q: Do you pay taxes?

A: <u>Yes.</u>

Military Service

Q: **Have you ever** left the United States to avoid being drafted into the U.S. Armed Forces? OR

            Have you ever left the United States so you didn't have to fight in a war?

Q: **Have you ever** applied for any kind of exemption from military service in the U.S. Armed Forces?

Q: **Have you ever** deserted from the U.S. Armed Forces?

Q: **Have you ever** failed to comply with Selective Service laws?

Q: **Have you ever** tried to avoid military service?

A: <u>No.</u>

Removal, Exclusion, and Deportation Proceedings

Q: Are removal, exclusion, rescission, or deportation proceedings pending against you?

Q: **Have you ever** been removed, excluded, or deported from the United States?

Q: **Have you ever** been ordered to be removed, excluded, or deported from the United States?

Q: **Have you ever** applied for any kind of relief from removal, exclusion, or deportation?

A: <u>No.</u>

Criminal Record

Q: **Have you ever** committed a crime or offense for which you were not arrested?

Q: **Have you ever** been arrested, cited, or detained by any law enforcement officer?

Q: **Have you ever** been charged with committing any crime or offense?

Q: **Have you ever** been placed in an alternative sentencing or a rehabilitative program?

Q: **Have you ever** received a suspended sentence, been placed on probation, or been paroled?

Q: **Have you ever** been in jail or prison?

Q: **Have you ever** lied to any U.S. government official?

A: <u>No.</u> (If you have ever been arrested, say "yes," and explain why.)

Good Moral Character

These questions ask about your moral character. The answers to these questions are usually "no," but be sure to understand what each question is asking. Read them carefully and learn the definitions of the key words that follow.

Q: Have you ever been a **habitual drunkard**? OR
Were you ever drunk every day?

A: <u>No, I drink only a little.</u> OR
<u>No, I don't drink alcohol.</u>

Q: Have you ever advocated or practiced **polygamy**? OR
Have you ever been married to more than one person at the same time?

A: <u>No.</u>

Q: Have you ever been a **prostitute**? OR
Have you ever sold your body for money?

A: <u>No, I've never taken money for sex.</u>

Q: Have you ever knowingly and for gain helped any alien to enter the United States illegally? OR
Have you ever smuggled anyone into the United States? OR
Have you ever accepted money for sneaking someone into the United States?

A: <u>No, I have never helped anyone enter the United States illegally.</u>

Q: Have you ever bought or sold illegal **drugs**? OR
              Have you ever been a trafficker in illegal drugs? OR
              Have you ever carried illegal drugs for someone else? OR
              Have you ever been a trafficker in cocaine or crack? OR
              Have you ever bought or sold marijuana or speed?
A: <u>No, I have never bought or sold illegal drugs.</u>

Q: Have you ever received income from illegal **gambling**? OR
              Did you ever get money illegally from gambling? OR
              Have you ever received money from illegal gambling? OR
              Have you ever received money or other goods from illegal
              gambling?
A: <u>No, I don't gamble.</u>

These last six questions will almost certainly be asked at your interview,
because they are the requirements for the Oath of Allegiance to the
United States. The answer to all of these questions should be "yes" if you
want to become an American citizen, but be sure you know what each
question means. Study the questions and vocabulary, and then read the
full Oath of Allegiance that follows. If you pass your interview, the interviewer will ask you to read the Oath of Allegiance and sign your name.

Q: 1. Do you support the **Constitution** and form of govern-
                  ment of the United States?
              2. Do you understand the full **Oath of Allegiance** to the
                  United States?
              3. Are you willing to take the full Oath of Allegiance to
                  the United States?
              4. If the law requires it, are you willing to **bear arms** on
                  behalf of the United States?
              5. If the law requires it, are you willing to perform **non-
                  combatant services** in the U.S. Armed Forces?
              6. If the law requires it, are you willing to perform work
                  of national importance under civilian direction?
A: <u>Yes.</u>

Oath of Allegiance

I hereby declare, on oath, that I absolutely and entirely renounce and abjure all allegiance and fidelity to any foreign prince, potentate, state, or sovereignty, of whom or which I have heretofore been a subject or citizen; that I will support and defend the Constitution and laws of the United States when required by law; that I will bear true faith and allegiance to the same; that I will bear arms on behalf of the United States when required by law; that I will perform noncombatant service in the Armed Forces of the United States when required by law; that I will perform work of national importance under civilian direction when required by law; and that I take this obligation freely, without any mental reservation or purpose of evasion; so help me God.

Language and Knowledge Assessment

During your interview, you will also be asked to show that you can read and write basic English. This is to ensure that you can listen to English, understand it, and write it. You will also be tested on basic U.S. history and civics from the 100 questions covered in Chapter 6.

100 Questions

Your interviewer will also ask you **ten** U.S. History and Civics questions from the list of 100 questions. You must answer **six** of these questions correctly to pass. Chapter 6 covers everything you need to know to answer these questions.

Dictation

After you answer ten questions, the interviewer will read you one sentence—probably from the list of dictation sentences—and he or she will ask you to write it down on the provided paper. The sentence is usually repeated at least three times. Practice writing from the list of sentences that follow. Practice writing each sentence on the line below the sentence. Have a friend or family member read the sentence out loud to you and then write it down carefully.

1.   I love living in the United States.

   _____

2.   I study English.

   _____

3.   I study citizenship.

   _____

4.   I want to be a citizen.

   _____

5.   I want to be an American.

   _____

6.   I live in New York City.

   _____

7.   I live with my big family.

   _____

8.   The president lives in the White House.

   _____

9.   I want to become an American citizen.

   _____

10.   I want to be a citizen of the United States.

   _____

11.   I want to live near my brother.

   _____

12.   I drive to work every day.

   _____

13.   His wife works at home.

   _____

14.   She works very hard at her job.

   _____

15.   Their children go to school every morning.

_____

16.   My daughter likes her teacher.

_____

17.   My sons want to go to college.

_____

18.   My family is happy to be in America.

_____

19.   We believe in freedom.

_____

20.   I believe in the Constitution.

_____

21.   I believe in freedom and the Constitution.

_____

22.   America is the land of the free.

_____

23.   America is the home of the brave.

_____

24.   I have four children.

_____

25.   I hope my children will be happy in America.

_____

26.   I live with my children and my husband.

_____

27.   We have a new home and we are a happy family.

_____

28.   America is the land of freedom.

_____

29.   Many people come to America for freedom.

_____

30.   It is important for all citizens to vote.

_____

31.   Congress passes laws in the United States.

_____

32.   The American flag has stars and stripes.

_____

33.   Citizens of the United States have the right to vote.

_____

34.   The people have a voice in government.

_____

35.   I want to be a citizen because I love America.

_____

36.   The Statue of Liberty was a gift from France.

_____

37.   Our government is divided into three branches.

_____

38.   Congress meets in Washington, D.C.

_____

39.   The president enforces the laws.

_____

40.   George Washington was the first American president.

_____

41.   The colors of the American flag are red, white, and blue.

_____

42.   The stars of the American flag are white.

_____

43.   The United States of America has 50 states.

_____

44.   Only Congress can declare war.

_____

45.   People vote for the president in November.

_____

46.   I studied for my citizenship exam with a book.

_____

47.   I studied for my citizenship exam on my own.

_____

48.   I studied for my citizenship exam in a class.

_____

49.   All students in my class will be taking a citizenship exam.

_____

50.   I want to become an American so I can vote.

_____

Reading

Next, the interviewer will show you a sentence and ask you to read it out loud. Practice reading from the list of sentences that follow. (These sentences are taken from the USCIS website, www.uscis.gov/graphics/services/natz/natzsamp.htm.)

Civics/History

A senator is elected for six years.

All people want to be free.

America is the land of freedom.

All U.S. citizens have the right to vote.

America is the home of the brave.

America is the land of the free.

Citizens have the right to vote.

Congress is part of the American government.

Congress meets in Washington, D.C.

Congress passes laws in the United States.

George Washington was the first president.

I want to be a citizen of the United States.

I want to be an American citizen.

I want to become an American so I can vote.

It is important for all citizens to vote.

Many people come to America for freedom.

Many people have died for freedom.

Martha Washington was the first First Lady.

Only Congress can declare war.

Our government is divided into three branches.

People in America have the right to freedom.

People vote for the president in November.

The American flag has stars and stripes.

The American flag has 13 stripes.

The capital of the United States is Washington, D.C.

The colors of the flag are red, white, and blue.

The Constitution is the supreme law of our land.

The flag of the United States has 50 stars.

The House and Senate are parts of Congress.

The people have a voice in government.

The people in the class took a citizenship test.

The president enforces the laws.

The president has the power of veto.

The president is elected every four years.

The president lives in the White House.

The president lives in Washington, D.C.

The president must be an American citizen.

The president must be born in the United States.

The president signs bills into law.

The stars of the American flag are white.

The Statue of Liberty was a gift from France.

The stripes of the American flag are red and white.

The White House is in Washington, D.C.

The United States of America has 50 states.

There are 50 states in the Union.

There are three branches of government.

Everyday Life

He came to live with his brother.

He has a very big dog.

She knows how to ride a bike.

He wanted to find a job.

She wanted to talk to her boss.

He went to the post office.

His wife is at work right now.

His wife worked in the house.

I am too busy to talk today.

I bought a blue car today.

I came to _____ (city) today for my interview.

I count the cars as they pass by the office.

I drive a blue car to work.

I go to work every day.

I have three children.

I know how to speak English.

I live in the state of _____.

I want to be a U.S. citizen.

It is a good job to start with.

My car does not work.

She can speak English very well.

She cooks for her friends.

She is my daughter, and he is my son.

He needs to buy some new clothes.

He wanted to live near his brother.

She was happy with her house.

The boy threw a ball.

The children bought a newspaper.

The children play at school.

The children wanted a television.

The man wanted to get a job.

The teacher was proud of her class.

The red house has a big tree.

They are a very happy family.

They are very happy with their car.

They buy many things at the store.

They came to live in the United States.

They go to the grocery store.

They have horses on their farm.

They live together in a big house.

They work well together.

Today, I am going to the store.

Today is a sunny day.

Warm clothing was on sale in the store.

We have a very clean house.

You cook very well.

You drink too much coffee.

You work very hard at your job.

Review

Remember the three useful phrases, and be sure that you can answer all of the following questions. Review this section if you need help.

Useful Phrases
◆ Please repeat that.
◆ Please speak more slowly.
◆ Please speak louder.

Greetings and Small Talk
◆ How are you?
◆ What is the weather like today? / How is the weather?
◆ What did you have for breakfast this morning?
◆ How did you get here today? / Who came with you?
◆ What day of the week is today?
◆ Do you know why you are here today?
◆ Why do you want to be a U.S. citizen?
◆ Do you have any questions before we begin?
◆ Have you studied for the citizenship test? What did you do?

Time Questions
◆ When did you first come to the United States?
◆ How long have you been a permanent resident?
◆ When was your last trip out of the United States?
◆ How long were you gone?
◆ How long have you lived at (current address)?
◆ How long have you worked at (current job)?

Place Questions
◆ Where did you first enter the United States? / What is your port of entry?
◆ What is your country of nationality?
◆ What is your country of birth? / Where were you born?

"Have You Ever" Questions

- ◆ Have you ever failed to file a tax return?
- ◆ Have you ever been part of the Communist Party / a terrorist organization?
- ◆ Have you ever been arrested, indicted, or convicted of a crime?
- ◆ Another way to categorize these questions is by question word. Listen carefully to the first word of each question and the key words in the question. Ask your interviewer to repeat if you did not hear it the first time.

"What" Questions

- ◆ **What** is your name?
- ◆ **What** is your Social Security number?
- ◆ **What** is your home telephone number?
- ◆ **What** is your date of birth?
- ◆ **What** is your marital status?
- ◆ **What** is your nationality?
- ◆ **What** is your height / weight / eye color / hair color?
- ◆ **What** is your address?
- ◆ **What** is your wife's / husband's name?
- ◆ **What** is his / her immigration status?

"How" Questions

- ◆ **How** are you?
- ◆ **How** is the weather?
- ◆ **How** did you get here?
- ◆ **How** do you spell your last name?

"How Long" Questions

- ◆ **How long** have you been a permanent resident?
- ◆ **How long** have you lived at (current address)?
- ◆ **How long** have you worked at (current job)?
- ◆ **How long** did the trip outside the United States last?
- ◆ **How long** have you been married?

"Where" Questions
- **Where** were you born?
- **Where** do you live?
- **Where** do you work?
- **Where** did you go (when you last left the United States)?
- **Where** were your children born?

"When" Questions
- **When** were you born?
- **When** did you come to the United States?
- **When** did you get your Permanent Resident Card?
- **When** did you get married?
- **When** did your spouse become a citizen?
- **When** did you move to (current address)?
- **When** was your last trip outside the United States?
- **When** did you return?
- **When** were your children born?

"Why" Questions
- **Why** do you want to become a citizen?
- **Why** were you out of the country for six months or longer?
- **Why** did you get divorced?
- **Why** aren't you working?

When the Exam Is Over

Some examiners will tell you that you passed when they have completed the exam. This is terrific news—you will know that all of your hard work has paid off. Then, you can prepare for your swearing-in ceremony.

If you should fail the exam, the USCIS examiner will suggest that you retake it. Often, the USCIS examiner will simply thank you for coming in, and tell you that you will receive notification of passing the exam in the mail. According to the law, the USCIS must grant or deny your application within 120 days after the interview. If you are denied because of failure of part of the exam, either English language or U.S.

history, you will get another chance to take the exam. However, if you miss the second appointment to retake the test, your application will be denied and you will have to start the whole process all over again.

Once your application is approved, your file gets updated in the USCIS database. Next, you will receive a certificate and a notice to appear at an Oath of Allegiance (swearing-in) Ceremony. Sometimes, the ceremony is at a courthouse; sometimes, it's at the USCIS office. Either way, it's official—you will be a U.S. citizen!

So, as you can see, it's very important to study and be well prepared on exam day. We have provided you with many sample questions in this chapter from which to study. The next chapter provides you with the complete list of official USCIS questions. Practice these two chapters frequently as you wait for your interview, and stick to your study schedule.

☆ ☆ ☆
SASHA'S STORY

I CAME to the United States from Yugoslavia in late 1991, during the early stages of the turmoil in my homeland. I was born in the republic of Serbia, in a small city very near Hungary. In the late 1980s when I was old enough to be drafted into the military, I was at university, so I was kept out of active duty. I studied computer science and hoped to make a life for myself outside of Yugoslavia. I went to a career fair in Belgrade, and I got a position in the Philippines with a major U.S. corporation. I viewed this as a strategic career move, because ultimately I wanted to live in the United States.

After two years, I was transferred to New York, where I worked long hours, learned advanced English, and quickly adapted to the American lifestyle. I made a lot of friends, mostly other Europeans. During this period, I learned so much about computer technology, which helped me to keep advancing my career. The corporation's attorneys secured my green card and started my process of naturalization. My passport is not honored in some countries because I am from Serbia, and while I am very proud of my heritage, I realized that to travel with ease, I had to become a U.S. citizen.

Becoming a citizen was a hard decision for me to make. Right outside of New York City, the climate and scenery looks remarkably similar to Serbia. Sometimes, I feel nostalgic for my homeland; other times, especially when I read negative headlines in the newspapers, I feel relieved that I am removed from the discord and violence back home.

In the middle of the naturalization process, another company offered me a job that I couldn't refuse. Unfortunately, this created a setback, as I had to not only deal with USCIS red tape, but also my former employers, who were slow in sending my naturalization paperwork to me after I left the company.

Because I was so busy with work, I ended up hiring an immigration attorney to help me with the rest of the process. Still, it took four years for my naturalization process to be complete. Last summer, I finally took the citizenship exam, which consisted of about 20 questions that seemed very much alike. I was glad I studied the civics portion, and I wasn't too worried about the language section because I had been in the States for ten years by that point, and I speak and understand English quite well. I was surprised to see so many people at my Oath Ceremony in New Jersey, and glad to find that I am happy in my adopted country. Now, I can travel back home, visit my family and friends, and travel freely in other European countries with the ease of an American.

☆ ☆ ☆

Words and Terms to Know

This list contains important citizenship terms and their definitions. Study this list to learn what each word means. Being familiar with these words will help you pass the citizenship exam.

Word	What It Means
A	
abolish	to destroy completely
address	where you live
adopted	put into effect
advise	to give help to
affiliated	linked or connected
alienage	status of being a foreign-born resident
allies	friends during war time
amendments	changes

appointed	chosen or selected
arrested	formally charged by a police officer
asylum	protection and immunity from extradition granted by a government to a political refugee from another country

B

banner	flag
basic belief	main idea, most important part
bear arms	carry a gun or weapon
benefits	good things, advantages
Bill of Rights	first ten amendments of the Constitution that tell the rights you have
birth place	country where you were born
born	when a baby comes into the world
branches	separate parts

C

cabinet	14 people who help the president make decisions
capital	city where the government is located
Capitol	where Congress meets
chief justice	head of the Supreme Court
citizen	a native, inhabitant, or denizen of a particular place
citizenship	the country where you have the right to fully participate in the benefits and laws of that country
civil rights leader	person who helps others believe in justice for all races of people
Civil War	war between the North and South
claimed	said something was true; pretended
colonies	original 13 states in America
Communist	person who belongs to a party that wants common ownership of property
Congress	people who make our laws
conscientious objections	reasons a person will not fight in a war
Constitution	supreme law of the United States
crime	breaking the law

D

Declaration of Independence	written statement saying the colonies wanted to be free from England
democracy	government of, by, and for the people
democratic republic	the form of the U.S. government
deported	a judge in court ordered you to go back to your first country
deserted	left the military without permission
different	another
drafted	ordered to be a soldier

E

Electoral College — group who elects the president

Emancipation Proclamation — written statement of freedom

employer — the name of the company or person you work for

enemies — people we fight in a war

executive branch — the part of the government made up of the president, vice president, and cabinet

exemption — to stay out of

explain — to give detailed information

F, G, H

false testimony — tell a lie

gamble — play games for money

governor — leader of a state

head executive — the leader or person in charge

habitual drunkard — person who drinks too much alcohol

I

illegal — against the law

inaugurated — sworn into office

income tax — if you work in America, this is the money you pay to the government

incompetent — not mentally capable; unskilled

independence — freedom

Independence Day — July 4th

interpret — to explain

introduction — the beginning

J, L

job — work or duty

judicial branch — the part of the government that includes the Supreme Court

legislative branch — Congress

liberty — freedom

M

maiden name — a woman's last name before getting married

marital status — if you are single, married, or divorced

mayor — leader of a city

mental institution — hospital for people who are mentally disabled

minimum — the lowest number allowed

N

national anthem — song about America

national importance — helpful to the United States

Native Americans	people who lived in America when the pilgrims arrived
natural born citizen	person who is born in a country
noncombatant service	help the military but not fight

O

oath	promise to tell the truth
Oath of Allegiance	officially swear to help the United States
occupation	the name of your job

P

passport	an official government document that certifies one's identity and citizenship and permits a citizen to travel abroad
persecution	hurt someone because of their race, religion, national origin, or political opinion
Pilgrims	people who came to America on a ship called the Mayflower
political party	group with similar ideas about government
polygamy	having more than one husband or wife at the same time
port of entry	place where you arrived in the country
preamble	the introduction to the Constitution
prostitute	a person who sells his or her body for money

R

reelected	voted into office again
registered	officially signed up to do something
represent	to stand for
representatives	people who work in the House of Representatives
Revolutionary War	war between the 13 colonies and England

S

senators	people who work in the Senate
slave	someone who is owned by another person
smuggle	to illegally sneak someone or something into the country
Supreme Court	highest court in the United States

T

term	how long someone works in government
tried	put through a trial with a judge and jury

U, W

union	United States of America
united	together as one
warrant	official permission from a judge
White House	place where president lives while serving as president

CHAPTER 5

U.S. History and Civics

WHEN YOU APPEAR for your interview, the USCIS interviewer will ask you specific U.S. history and civics questions. You will see examples of these questions in Chapter 6. In order to be more confident during the oral exam, it is a good idea to understand the *context* of the questions being asked. In this chapter, you are provided with a brief overview of the areas of U.S. history that the exam covers. Reading over the history of the United States is a really good way to supplement your exam preparation. Of course, you can just memorize questions and sample answers if that works for you, but we urge you to read on—you will discover many interesting facts about your new country. Plus, we've added some interesting pieces of information to help you as you study early U.S. history—from the discovery of the Americas through the civil war, to some basic and necessary facts on U.S. government.

☆ **CONTEXT:** the circumstances in which an event occurs; a setting

Key Presidents

All of our past presidents are important for one reason or another, but you are most likely to be asked about these four presidents:

- ◆ The first president of the United States was George Washington.
- ◆ The president who wrote the Declaration of Independence was Thomas Jefferson.
- ◆ The president who ended slavery was Abraham Lincoln.
- ◆ The current president of the United States is George W. Bush. (This was true at the time this book was published.)

☆ ☆ ☆

It Happened In . . .

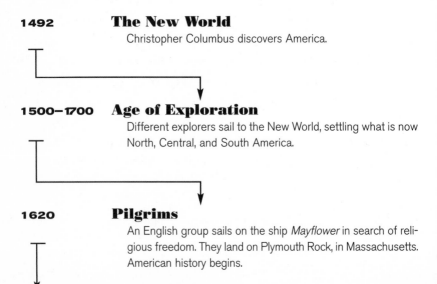

1492 **The New World**
Christopher Columbus discovers America.

1500–1700 **Age of Exploration**
Different explorers sail to the New World, settling what is now North, Central, and South America.

1620 **Pilgrims**
An English group sails on the ship *Mayflower* in search of religious freedom. They land on Plymouth Rock, in Massachusetts. American history begins.

Mayflower Compact

The pilgrims drafted a document that outlined the first form of government in the New World. The U.S. Constitution is based on the principles from this document.

Thanksgiving

After a successful first harvest based on the Native Americans' method of farming, the first Thanksgiving is celebrated.

1660–1770s # The British Colonies in America

The English governed the American colonies. The American colonies relied on England for trade, and the English were pleased to have a growing market in America. During this time, more settlers crossed the Atlantic Ocean from England, as well as from Ireland, France, Holland, Germany, and Spain. The population grew, and 13 distinct colonies were incorporated and governed by the English. The northern colonies became areas of smaller farms, commercial businesses, and some manufacturing ventures. The southern colonies, with vast land and warm climate, were more suitable for farming on a larger scale. Plantations were formed, farming "cash crops"—tobacco, sugar, and cotton.

1740 ## Slavery

In order to farm the large plantations in the South, slaves were brought to the colonies from Africa.

1752–1763 # The French and Indian War

The French, with the aid of the Native Americans who did not appreciate the British taking over their land, battled the British on American soil.

1763–1775   Taxation without Representation

The British were heavily taxing the colonial settlers, and the British governors started to get more involved in the daily lives of the colonists. **Patrick Henry,** an outspoken colonist, opposed taxation, especially the **Stamp Act of 1765.** He gave a famous speech that ended with, **"Give me liberty or give me death!"** Representatives from each of the 13 colonies gathered in Philadelphia to discuss their problem with the British. This important meeting became known as **"The First Continental Congress"** of September 1774. The representatives drafted and sent a petition known as the **"Declaration of Rights"** to King George of England. In the Declaration of Rights, the colonists asked for specific changes in the treatment of the colonies by the British. The colonists wanted tax relief, representation in British parliament, and greater freedom.

1775   "The Shot Heard 'Round the World"

Famous incidents occurred in and around Boston, such as the **Boston Tea Party,** where colonists dumped British tea (an item that was heavily taxed) into Boston Harbor. This represented the colonists' intolerance of taxes by the British. They coined a slogan, "No taxation without representation," and angered England. The British troops began shooting the colonists. **Paul Revere** warned the settlers of the troops' approach by riding through the areas around Boston, shouting, "The British are coming! The British are coming!" The colonists challenged England's absolute rule, and the enemies of England, such as the French, rallied behind the colonies. This began the **Revolutionary War.**

1776   The Declaration of Independence

The Second Continental Congress met in Philadelphia on July 4, 1776. During this meeting, the representatives from the 13 colonies drafted *The Declaration of Independence,* written by **Thomas Jefferson,** and elected **George Washington** as commander in chief of the Continental Armed Forces. The colonies renamed themselves the "United States of America."

1776–1783   # The Articles of Confederation

The representatives of the 13 states realized that they need-ed a governing document. They drafted *The Articles of Confederation,* a temporary outline of the principles of gov-ernment for the United States of America. It would serve as the guiding principles for the young nation until the *U.S. Constitution* was written.

The U.S. Constitution

After the Revolutionary War, the thirteen states realized that the loose form or *The Articles of Confederation,* which gave the federal government very little power and had no provi-sion for taxes, would not work. They came back to Philadel-phia and wrote *The U.S. Constitution.* Each state had to ratify, or agree with, the new laws, and it passed unani-mously in 1789.

1789–1860   # The Great Expansion

With westward expansion came an era of prosperity in the United States. The northern states began to abolish slavery, while slavery continued in the South. This issue, among oth-ers, divided the young nation.

1860–1865   # The Civil War

The War Between the States was the bloodiest war fought on American soil, and it resulted in more American casualties than any war since.

1865   # End of Slavery

With the end of the war and victory for the North, President Abraham Lincoln ended slavery. In April, Lincoln was shot and killed.

☆

Thanksgiving

The U.S. holiday celebrated on the last Thursday in November commemorates the first harvest that the Pilgrims had with the Native Americans in the New World. The original settlers gave thanks for the bountiful food as well as the peace and freedom they enjoyed in their new homeland. Turkey is served as the main course because it is a bird native to North America. Other unique foods include corn and cranberries—new vegetables and fruit found in the New World.

The Original 13 Colonies

Massachusetts
New Hampshire
Rhode Island
Connecticut
New York
New Jersey
Pennsylvania
Delaware
Maryland
Virginia
North Carolina
South Carolina
Georgia

Did You Know . . .

. . . that the first rules regarding the granting of national citizenship into the United States were established by the Act of March 26, 1790. This first federal naturalization law originally laid down two of the most basic and important principles of what would evolve into the modern laws of today—persons eligible for naturalization were required to have lived in the United States for a minimum period of time, and to have displayed a good moral character worthy of being a citizen of the United States.

The United States Constitution

The Constitution provided for a strong national government divided into three branches: legislative, judicial, and executive.

The Three Branches of Government

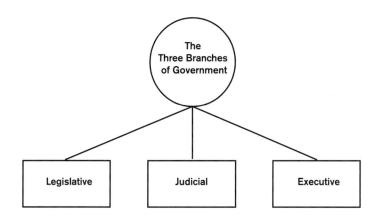

Legislative Branch

➤ The legislative branch of the government is called Congress.

➤ Congress makes the laws in the United States.

➤ Congress has two parts: the Senate and the House of Representatives.

➤ Members of Congress are voted into office by adult citizens of the United States.

➤ Congress meets at the Capitol in Washington, D.C.

➤ There are 100 senators in Congress—two from each state.

➤ A senator has a term in office of six years.

➤ There is no limit to how many times a senator can be reelected.

➤ There are 435 members of the House of Representatives. The number of representatives per state is based on population.

➤ Each representative is elected for a term of two years.

➤ There is no limit to how many times a representative can be reelected.

Judicial Branch

➤ The Supreme Court is the judicial branch of our government.

➤ The duty of the Supreme Court is to interpret laws and the Constitution.

➤ The chief justice of the Supreme Court is John G. Roberts.

➤ The president selects the Supreme Court justices, and Congress must approve his or her choices.

➤ There are nine Supreme Court justices.

➤ The Supreme Court is the highest court in the United States.

Executive Branch

➤ The executive branch of our government consists of the president, vice president, and members of the cabinet.

➤ The president of the United States is elected for a four-year term.

➤ If the president of the United States dies in office, the vice president becomes the president.

➤ A president can serve a maximum of two terms, and he or she must win the vote of the Electoral College—not just the popular vote of the adult citizens of the United States.

➤ The Speaker of the House of Representatives becomes president if the president and vice president die.

➤ To be eligible for president, one must be a natural-born citizen of the United States, at least 35 years old, and have lived in the United States for at least 14 years.

➤ The president lives at the White House: 1600 Pennsylvania Avenue, Washington, D.C.

➤ The chief executive of a state is the governor.

➤ The chief executive of a city is the mayor.

Facts to Know about the U.S. Constitution

1. The Constitution is the supreme law of the United States of America.
2. It was written in 1787.
3. It can only be changed by an act in Congress. Changes to the Constitution are called amendments.
4. There are 27 amendments to the Constitution.
5. The first ten amendments are called the Bill of Rights.
6. The introduction to the Constitution is called the preamble.
7. Some rights and freedoms granted by the Bill of Rights are:
   ◆ The freedoms of speech, press, and religion.
   ◆ The right of all adult citizens 18 years of age and over to vote and the right to bear arms.
   ◆ Government may not put soldiers in people's homes, search or take a person's property without a warrant.
   ◆ A person may not be tried for the same crime twice, and a person charged with a crime has rights, including the right to a trial and a lawyer.
   ◆ People are protected from unreasonable fines or cruel punishment.

The American Flag

◆ The colors of the American flag are red, white, and blue.
◆ There are 50 white stars on a blue background, and they represent the 50 states.
◆ There are 13 red and white stripes on the flag, representing the 13 original colonies.

Know Your State

(Fill in the blanks and study this information about your local government.)

1. What is the capital of your state? _____
2. Who is the governor of your state? _____
3. Who is the mayor of your city or town? _____

The United States Today

◆ The capital of the United States is Washington, D.C.
◆ The United States is a democratic republic.

Supplemental Reading Materials

As a citizen of the United States, it's important to understand the history of our great nation. The ten books listed below will not only supplement your studies for the citizenship exam, but they will also give you a broad knowledge of American history and a better idea of how the country works. Each book offers something different, and all are interesting and easy to read. When you have spare time, head to your local library or bookstore and see which one is right for you.

Twenty-Five Lessons in Citizenship, by D.L. Hennessey and Lenore Hennessey Richardson (D.L. Hennessey, 1997).

Voices of Freedom: English and Civics for the U.S. Citizenship Exam, by Bill Bliss with Steven J. Molinsky (Simon & Schuster, 1993).

Making Patriots, by Walter Berns (University of Chicago Press, 2001).

"To the Best of My Ability": The American Presidents, edited by James M. McPherson and David Rubel (Dorling Kindersley, 2000).

A People's History of the United States: 1492–Present, by Howard Zinn (HarperTrade, 1995).

Witness to America: An Illustrated Documentary History of the United States from the Revolution to Today (includes audio CD), edited by Stephen E. Ambrose (HarperCollins, 1999).

The Limits of Liberty: American History, 1607–1992, by Maldwyn Allen Jones (Oxford University Press, 1995).

The Great Republic: A History of the United States, by Winston S. Churchill (Random House, 1999).

What Every American Should Know about American History: 200 Events That Shaped the Nation, by Alan Axelrod and Charles Phillips (Adams, 1993).

The American Flag, by Patricia Ryon Quiri (Children's Press, 1998).

Learning Online

The Internet can be an invaluable learning and research tool. Here is a list of websites that will supplement your studies for the oral interview. If you have a specific question or want to learn more about a subject, simply go to a site, and perform a search. (*Note:* At the time of publication, the websites listed here were current. Due to the ever-changing nature of the Web, we cannot guarantee their continued existence or content.)

History Channel Online
  www.history.com

U.S.A. History.com
  www.usahistory.com

Encyclopedia Britannica Online
  www.britannica.com

History.org
  www.ushistory.org

Great Books Online
  www.bartleby.com

50 States and Capitals
  www.50states.com

The White House Homepage
  www.whitehouse.gov

Grolier Online's The American Presidency
  http://ap.grolier.com

American Memory: Historical Collections for the National Digital Library
  http://memory.loc.gov/

United States of America National Anthem:
The Star-Spangled Banner
by Francis Scott Key, 1814

Oh say can you see, by the dawn's early light,
What so proudly we hail'd at the twilight's last gleaming?
Whose broad stripes and bright stars, thro' the perilous fight,
O'er the ramparts we watch'd were so gallantly streaming?
And the rocket's red glare, the bombs bursting in air,
Gave proof thro' the night that our flag was still there.
O say, does that Star Spangled Banner yet wave
O'er the land of the free and the home of the brave?

On the shore dimly seen throughout the mists of the deep
Where the foe's haughty host in dread silence reposes
What is that which the breeze o'er the towering steep
As it fitfully blows, half conceals, half discloses?
Now it catches the gleam of the morning's first beam
In full glory reflected now shines on the stream.
'Tis the Star Spangled Banner, Oh long may it wave
O'er the land of the free and the home of the brave.

And where is that band who so hauntingly swore
That the havoc of war and the battle's confusion
A home and country, shall leave us no more?
Their blood was washed out their foul foot steps pollution
No refuge could save the hireling and slave
From the terror of flight or the gloom of the grave.
And the Star Spangled Banner in triumph doth wave
O'er the land of the free and the home of the brave.

Oh thus be it e'er when free men shall stand
Between their lov'd homes and war's desolation!
Blest with vict'ry and peace, may the heav'n rescued land
Praise the Pow'r that has made and preserv'd us as a nation
And conquer we must when our cause is just
And this be our motto: "In God is our trust."
And the Star Spangled banner in triumph shall wave
O'er the land of the free and the home of the brave.

CHAPTER 6

Official USCIS Questions and Sample Answers

HERE IS A list, arranged by category, of all the official USCIS history and civics questions and answers. You need to know the answers to many of these questions to pass the test. Cover the answers and try to answer each question correctly. Then look at the answers to see if you are correct. Or, study with a friend. Have your friend ask you the questions and you respond aloud. Keep track of how many you answer correctly. If you need extra help with the answers, go back to Chapter 5 for our basic U.S. Civics lesson.

Flash Cards

Here's a fun and effective study idea—create flash cards to help you learn the official USCIS questions and answers. It's simple:

1. Buy index cards at your local stationery store, paper supplier, or drug store.
2. Write a USCIS question on one side of a card, and the correct answer on the back.

3. Shuffle the cards and have a friend or family member drill you on the questions.
4. Keep trying until you get them all right!

The Government Structure

1. How many branches are there in the government?

   1. Three (3)

2. What are the three branches of our government?

   2. Executive, legislative, and judicial

Legislative Branch

3. What is the legislative branch of our government?

   3. Congress

4. Who makes the laws in the United States?

   4. Congress

5. What is Congress?

   5. The Senate and House of Representatives

6. What are the duties of Congress?

   6. To make laws

7. Who elects the members of Congress?

   7. The voting citizens of the United States

8. Where does Congress meet?

   8. The Capitol in Washington, D.C.

9. How many senators are there in Congress?

   9. One hundred (100)

10. Why are there 100 senators in Congress?

    10. There are two (2) senators from each of the 50 states.

11. Who are the two senators from your state?

    11. Each state has a different answer. Find out who are the two senators from your state.

12. How long is an elected senator's term?

    12. Six (6) years for each term he or she is elected

13. How many times can a senator be reelected?

    13. There is no limit.

14. How many representatives are there in Congress?

    14. Four hundred thirty-five (435)

15. How long is an elected representative's term?

    15. *Two (2) years for each term he or she is elected*

16. How many times can a representative be reelected?

    16. *There is no limit.*

Judicial Branch

17. What is the judicial branch of our government?

    17. *The Supreme Court*

18. What are the duties of the Supreme Court?

    18. *To interpret laws and the Constitution*

19. Who is the chief justice of the Supreme Court?

    19. *John Roberts*

20. Who selects the Supreme Court justices?

    20. *The president*

21. How many Supreme Court justices are there?

    21. *Nine (9)*

22. What is the highest court in the United States?

    22. *The Supreme Court*

Executive Branch

23. What is the executive branch of our government?

    23. *The president, vice president, and cabinet*

24. Who was the first president of the United States?

    24. *George Washington*

25. Who is the president of the United States today?

    25. *George W. Bush*

26. Who is the vice president today?

    26. *Richard Cheney*

27. Who elects the president of the United States?

    27. *The Electoral College*

28. How long is an elected president's term?

    28. *Four (4) years*

29. Who becomes president of the United States if the president should die?

    29. *The vice president*

30. How many terms can a president serve?

30. *A maximum of two (2) terms*

31. Who becomes president of the United States if the president and vice president should die?

31. *The Speaker of the House of Representatives*

32. What are the requirements to be president?

32. *The president must be a natural-born citizen of the United States, at least thirty-five (35) years old, and have lived in the United States for at least fourteen (14) years.*

33. What special group advises the president?

33. *The cabinet*

34. What is the White House?

34. *The president's official home*

35. Where is the White House located?

35. *1600 Pennsylvania Avenue, Washington, D.C.*

36. In what month do we vote for the president?

36. *November*

37. In what month is the new president inaugurated?

37. *January*

38. What is the head executive of a state government called?

38. *Governor*

39. What is the head executive of a city government called?

39. *Mayor*

40. Who signs a bill into law?

40. *The president*

41. What is the name of the president's official home?

41. *The White House*

42. Who is commander in chief of the U.S. military?

42. *The president*

43. Who has the power to declare war?

43. *Congress*

☆ **INAUGURATED:** inducted into office by a formal ceremony

The Constitution

44. What is the Constitution?

44. *The supreme law of the land*

45. Can the Constitution be changed?

45. *Yes*

46. What do we call changes made to the Constitution?

46. *Amendments*

47. How many amendments are there?

47. *Twenty-seven (27)*

48. What is the supreme law of the United States?

48. *The Constitution*

49. What year was the Constitution written?

49. *1787*

50. What is the Bill of Rights?

50. *The first ten (10) amendments*

51. Where does freedom of speech come from?

51. *The Bill of Rights*

52. Whose rights are guaranteed by the Constitution and the Bill of Rights?

52. *Everyone in the United States, including noncitizens*

53. What is the introduction to the Constitution called?

53. *The preamble*

54. What are the first ten amendments to the Constitution called?

54. *The Bill of Rights*

55. Name three rights or freedoms guaranteed by the Bill of Rights.

55. *1. The freedoms of speech, press, and religion 2. The right to bear arms 3. Government may not put soldiers in people's homes. 4. Government may not search or take a person's property without a warrant. 5. A person may not be tried for the same crime twice. 6. A person charged with a crime has* *rights, including the right to a trial and a lawyer. 7. People are protected from unreasonable fines or cruel punishment.*

56. Name one right guaranteed by the First Amendment.

56. *Freedom of speech, press, religion, peaceable assembly, and requesting change of government*

57. What is the most important right granted to U.S. citizens?

57. *The right to vote*

58. What is the minimum voting age in the United States?

58. *Eighteen (18) years old*

Did You Know . . .

. . . that 898,315 applicants for naturalization were approved and took the Oath of Allegiance in 2000.

United States History

59. What is the 4th of July?

59. *Independence Day*

60. On what date was the Declaration of Independence adopted?

60. *July 4, 1776*

61. What is the basic belief stated in the Declaration of Independence?

61. *All men are created equal.*

62. Who was the main writer of the Declaration of Independence?

62. *Thomas Jefferson*

63. What is the date of Independence Day?

63. *July 4th*

64. Which president was the first commander in chief of the U.S. military?

64. *George Washington*

65. What country did the United States gain its independence from?

65. *England*

66. What country did we fight during the Revolutionary War?

66. *England*

67. Who said, "Give me liberty or give me death"?

67. *Patrick Henry*

68. Which president is called the "father of our country"?

68. *George Washington*

69. Why did the Pilgrims come to America?

69. *They were seeking religious freedom.*

70. Who helped the Pilgrims in America?

70. *The Native Americans helped the Pilgrims.*

71. What ship brought the Pilgrims to America?

71. *The* Mayflower

72. What holiday was celebrated for the first time by the American colonists?

72. *Thanksgiving*

73. What were the original 13 states called?

73. *The original thirteen (13) states were called colonies.*

74. Can you name the original 13 states?

74. *Connecticut, New Hampshire, New York, New Jersey, Massachusetts, Pennsylvania, Delaware, Virginia, North Carolina, South Carolina, Georgia, Rhode Island, and Maryland*

75. Who wrote "The Star-Spangled Banner"?

75. *Francis Scott Key*

76. What is the national anthem of the United States?

76. *"The Star-Spangled Banner"*

77. Who was the president during the Civil War?

77. *Abraham Lincoln*

78. What did the Emancipation Proclamation do?

78. *The Emancipation Proclamation freed all slaves in the United States.*

79. Which president freed the slaves?

79. *Abraham Lincoln*

80. What are the 49th and 50th states in the union?

80. *Alaska and Hawaii*

81. Who were America's enemies in World War II?

81. *Germany, Japan, and Italy*

82. Who was Martin Luther King, Jr.?

82. *A civil rights leader in the 1960s*

The Flag

83. What are the colors of our flag?

83. *Red, white, and blue*

84. How many stars are on our flag?

84. *There are fifty (50) stars.*

85. What color are the stars on our flag?

85. *The stars are white.*

86. What do the stars on the flag represent?

86. *The fifty (50) states. There is one star for each state in the Union.*

87. How many stripes are on the flag?

87. *Thirteen (13)*

88. What color are the stripes on the flag?

88. *The stripes are red and white.*

89. What do the stripes on the flag represent?

89. *The original thirteen (13) colonies*

Your State Government

90. What is the capital of your state?

90. *Each state has a different answer. Find out the name of the capital of your state.*

91. Who is the current governor of your state?

91. *Each state has a different answer. Find out who is the governor of your state.*

92. Who is the head of your local government?

92. *Find out the name of your local mayor.*

The United States Today

93. How many states are there in the United States?

    93. *There are fifty (50) states.*

94. Name one purpose of the United Nations.

    94. *For countries to talk about world problems and try to peaceably solve them*

95. Name one benefit of becoming a citizen of the United States.

    95. *The right to vote, the right to travel with a U.S. passport, the right to serve on a jury, the right to apply for federal jobs*

96. What are the two major political parties in the U.S. today?

    96. *The Democratic and Republican parties*

97. What kind of government does the United States have?

    97. *A democratic republic*

98. What is the United States Capitol?

    98. *The place where Congress meets*

99. Where is the capital of the United States?

    99. *Washington, D.C.*

100. What USCIS form is used to apply to become a naturalized citizen?

    100. *Form N-400, the "Application to File Petition for Naturalization"*

Top Ten Metropolitan Areas of Intended Residence

In 2003, the following metropolitan areas were selected by the largest number of immigrants as their areas of intended residence:

New York, New York

Los Angeles/Long Beach, California

Chicago, Illinois

Metropolitan Washington, D.C.

Miami, Florida

Houston, Texas

Orange County, California

Oakland, California

Boston, Massachusetts

San Jose, California

Source: USCIS

Did You Know . . .

. . . If you have access to the Internet, you can print out USCIS civics flash cards or hear them read out loud at www.USCIS.gov/graphics/citizenship/flashcards.

☆ ☆ ☆

IMMIGRATION SPECIALIST JULIO DOMINGUEZ'S STORY

I was motivated to become a lawyer by events that occurred in my childhood. I was born in Bakersfield, California, shortly after my parents emigrated there from Mexico City. Growing up in a largely Hispanic community in southern California, the subjects of immigration and citizenship were always an issue amongst family and friends. From what I could see, my community lacked a really good lawyer to assist the hardworking people that desired citizenship. It seemed to me (and I viewed it firsthand when my father went through the naturalization process when I was a teen) that many of the so-called immigration specialists were stereotypical lawyer-types who were more interested in taking advantage than actually helping out. When I got to law school, I took an immigration law course and was also a student advocate in our school's immigration clinic. Working in the clinic helping out people from all over the world, it didn't take me long to realize that specializing in immigration was my calling.

I have been practicing law now for about ten years, nine of them concentrating in immigration law. I work for a small firm that specializes in corporate immigration cases. That pays my bills. In my spare time I like to go to back my community and work on private cases—my clients are usually Latin American or Mexican, and I often work pro bono—helping hardworking people like my parents is all the payment I need. On occasion, I will also conduct free information seminars at a local church. The naturalization process is actually quite simple if you know exactly what you're doing, and I try to be as helpful as possible.

In terms of things that I have noticed about both my corporate and private clients, the physical presence and Selective Service requirements seem to cause the most confusion. This is where having someone who knows the legal ins and outs can be very helpful. There are many things about the naturalization process that are discouraging to candidates, but they should know that every community has a number of people like me who are more than willing to help, because we know exactly where they are coming from.

Special Situations

HAVE YOU EVER heard someone say that for every rule there is an exception? Well, the United States government is no exception! In Chapter 2, you read about some exceptions in reference to the oral exam. Also, different rules apply to people with different status, such as marriage to an American citizen, or a U.S. military veteran. In this chapter, you will read about a few other situations that may affect your naturalization process.

Keeping Your Cool with the USCIS

Here are some important tips to remember when calling the USCIS or when you are at the USCIS office seeking information:

➤ <u>Be Persistent</u>—If the representative you speak with is not able to help you, call back or ask to be placed on hold while another person is found who might be helpful. The same rule applies in person—ask your representative to ask someone else in the office for assistance with your particular question. Call again or go back if you didn't get all the information you need.

➤ Stay Calm—It's always hard to understand what the other person is saying when you're upset. (This is true even if English is your native language!) Remain calm as you absorb the information.

➤ Be Polite—Representatives will be more helpful if you conduct yourself in a professional, courteous manner.

➤ Repeat Your Question—until you are understood.

➤ Repeat the USCIS Answer—until you understand it.

➤ Be Patient—All of the new citizens interviewed for this book told us that they were very frustrated when dealing with the USCIS. They became U.S. citizens, and so can you!

Alien Fiancé(e)s and Marriage

A common special situation regarding citizenship is when a U.S. citizen wishes to marry a non-U.S. citizen. Here are some basic steps to follow, but do visit the USCIS and other government websites regularly to confirm that these steps, rules, and regulations are current.

A citizen of a foreign country who would like to come to the United States to marry an American citizen and reside in the United States will have to obtain a K-1 visa. Since this book is about citizenship and not visas, this section will be brief. For more information on fiancé(e) visas or other types of visas, such as the student visa, you can e-mail usvisa@state.gov.

Briefly, to establish K-1 visa classification for an alien fiancé(e), a U.S. citizen must file a petition, Form I-129F, *Petition for Alien Fiancé(e)*, with the designated USCIS service center or at a U.S. consulate abroad, which will forward the petition to the appropriate USCIS office. These petitions cannot be filed or processed while abroad; they must be handled in the United States by the USCIS. The consular office where the alien fiancé(e) will apply for his or her visa will receive notification of the petition approval and issue a K-1 visa. A petition is valid for a period of four months from the date of USCIS action, and may be revalidated by the consular officer. The fiancé(e) must marry the U.S. citizen within 90 days of arriving in the United States.

Visa Ineligibility

Warning: Applicants who have a communicable disease, or have a dangerous physical or mental disorder; are drug addicts; have committed serious criminal acts, including crimes involving moral turpitude, drug trafficking, and prostitution; are likely to become a public charge; have used fraud or other illegal means to enter the United States; or are ineligible for citizenship, may be refused a visa. In limited circumstances, waivers for a ground of inadmissibility may be available.

Source: www.travel.state.gov/visa/frvi/ineligibilities/ineligibilities_1364.html

☆ **TURPITUDE:** a corrupt or degenerate act or practice

Applying for a Fiancé(e) Visa

The consular officer will notify the beneficiary (U.S. citizen fiancé(e)) when the approved petition is received, and the beneficiary will be provided with the necessary forms and instructions to apply for a K-1 class visa. A fiancé(e) visa applicant is intending to immigrate and, therefore, must meet documentary requirements similar to the requirements of an immigrant visa applicant. The following documents are normally required:

◆ Valid passport
◆ Birth certificate
◆ Divorce or death certificate of any previous spouse
◆ Police certificate from all places lived since age 16 for six months duration or longer
◆ Medical examination
◆ Evidence of financial support by fiancé(e)

◆ Evidence of valid relationship with the petitioner

◆ Photographs (like those required for naturalization)

Both petitioner (U.S. fiancé(e)) and beneficiary (alien fiancé(e)) must be legally able and willing to conclude a valid marriage in the United States. This may seem like an obvious point, but some people try to abuse the marriage route to U.S. citizenship because it is shorter. The petitioner and beneficiary must have previously met in person within the past two years unless the Attorney General waives that requirement. Again, this may seem like a strange rule for two people getting married, but it is there to prevent fraud. You may wonder why the Attorney General would waive this rule. Well, in some cases, such as when there has been war or military occupation, fiancé(e)s may have been separated from each other. This exception is in place to help people who are committed to the United States and to each other.

☆ **FRAUD:** a deception deliberately practiced in order to secure unfair or unlawful gain

As soon as the processing of the application is complete and the applicant has all necessary documents, a consular officer will interview the fiancé(e). If found eligible, a visa will be issued, valid for one entry during a period of six months. A nonrefundable $165 application fee is collected. For more about U.S. visas, visit these helpful websites:

www.travel.state.gov
www.USCIS.gov
www.usavisanow.com
www.k1-fiance-visa.com

After Entry into the United States

The alien fiancé(e) first may apply for work authorization with the USCIS. This is because the government wants to ensure that the new resident of the United States will be a productive part of the U.S. economy.

Next, the marriage must take place within 90 days of admission into the United States. Following the marriage, the alien spouse must apply to the USCIS for adjustment of status to Legal Permanent Residency (green card) by filing forms I-485 and I-130. If approved, the USCIS will grant a two-year conditional permanent residence status. After two years, the alien may apply to the USCIS for removal of the conditional status (Form I-751) by providing evidence that the marriage remains intact. At this point, the alien spouse is well on the road to U.S. citizenship.

Family Members

The unmarried, minor children of a fiancé(e) (K-1) beneficiary derive K-2 nonimmigrant visa status from the parent *if the children are named in the petition.* A separate petition is not required if the children accompany or follow the alien fiancé(e) within one year from the date of issuance of the K-1 visa. After one year, a separate immigrant visa petition is required.

Did You Know . . .

. . . a permanent resident spouse of a U.S. citizen can apply for naturalization after living three years in the United States, provided that he or she meets all physical, residence, and naturalization requirements. There are certain exceptions to this rule if the permanent resident is married to a citizen stationed or employed abroad by:

➤ the U.S. government (including the U.S. Armed Forces);

➤ American research institutes recognized by the Attorney General;

➤ recognized U.S. religious organizations;

➤ U.S. research institutions;

➤ an American firm engaged in the development of foreign trade and commerce of the United States; or certain public international organizations involving the United States.

If you think you might qualify for one of these exceptions, contact the USCIS for further information.

Source: U.S. Immigration and Naturalization Service, *A Guide to Naturalization,*
U.S. Government Printing Office: Washington, D.C., 2004

Unfortunately, the route to citizenship through marriage has been abused so much over the years that the U.S. government has purposely made the process more complicated, and ultimately, more confusing. If possible, try to speak to a legal advisor or somebody who has previously been through the process to avoid some of the legal snags in obtaining a K-1 visa.

Citizenship for Foreign-Born and Adopted Children of U.S. Citizens

If you are considering adoption, here is some important information to know in order to help you cut through the red tape. Adopted foreign-born children can become U.S. citizens either automatically (under the Child Citizenship Act of 2000) or by filing USCIS Form N-600 or N-600K before the child's 18th birthday. For more information, please see the USCIS website for fact sheets and proposed regulations.

Automatic Citizenship
Most foreign-born adopted children automatically become citizens on the date they immigrate to the United States. According to the USCIS, there are a few requirements that must be met in order for this to occur. These are:

◆ At least one adoptive parent must be a U.S. citizen
◆ The child must be under 18 years of age
◆ A full and final adoption of the child must be complete
◆ The child must be in the United States as a permanent resident or have an automatic Grant of Citizenship and Citizenship by Application if the child is living abroad

If all of these requirements are met, the child is automatically a U.S. citizen.

Applying for Citizenship for a Child
If the requirements for automatic citizenship are not met, the parent must apply for citizenship on the child's behalf. If the parent is a U.S. citizen, he or she will fill out a Form N-600.

If the parent is a permanent resident, not a U.S. citizen, he or she will apply for citizenship on behalf of the child **only** when applying for citizenship. In this case, the parent will fill out his or her application for naturalization as described earlier in this book, including Form N-600 with their application.

Remember, these procedures apply only to children under the age of 18. Adopted children who are 18 or older must apply for citizenship on their own behalf. They will follow the process described earlier, as well.

Did You Know . . .

. . . under the Child Citizenship Act of 2000, foreign-born children who currently reside in the United States and who meet certain requirements may automatically qualify for citizenship.

Children who automatically qualify for citizenship **do not** have to apply for it. They receive citizenship on the date they meet all of the requirements. They will not, however, automatically receive proof of citizenship. To receive proof, parents should apply for a Certificate of Citizenship with the USCIS. This certificate is needed to obtain a U.S. passport for their child from a local passport agency.

If both parents of a child born on foreign soil are U.S. citizens, and at least one of those parents lived in the United States prior to the child's birth, the child acquires U.S. citizenship. Parents should apply for a Certificate of Citizenship (Form N-600) for their child; this document is evidence of a child's citizenship, much like a birth certificate. Also, under the Child Citizen Act (CCA), a new law that went into effect on February 27, 2001, adopted children (under 18 years old) of U.S. citizens automatically acquire U.S. citizenship by operation of law the day they immigrate to the United States. If they live abroad, they need to apply for citizenship. This new law protects the adopted foreign-born children of U.S. citizens from deportation.

Dual Citizenship

When people say someone has dual citizenship, they mean that he or she is a citizen of two countries at the same time. Some people are born to parents with different nationalities, giving them dual citizenship. Some people retain citizenship of their home country when they become United States citizens.

Each country has its own citizenship laws and there are several that do not allow dual citizenship. The following is a list of countries that allow dual citizenship—excluding those with special regulations. It is based on the most current information available at the time of publication. You should check with your home country to see if it allows dual citizenship before you apply for naturalization.

Countries That Typically Recognize Dual Citizenship

Albania	Cyprus	Italy
Antigua & Barbuda	Cyprus (North)	Jamaica
Argentina	Dominica	Jordan
Australia	Dominican Republic	Latvia
Bahamas	Ecuador	Lebanon
Bangladesh	Egypt	Lesotho
Barbados	El Salvador	Liechtenstein
Belize	Fiji	Lithuania
Benin	France	Macao (with Portugal)
Bolivia	Germany	Macedonia
Brazil	Ghana	Madagascar
Bulgaria	Greece	Malta
Burkina Faso	Grenada	Mexico
Cambodia	Guatemala	Montenegro
Canada	Haiti	(Yugoslavia)
Cape Verde	Hungary	Mongolia
Chile	India	Morocco
Colombia	Iran	Netherlands
Costa Rica	Ireland	New Zealand
Croatia	Israel	Nicaragua

Nigeria	Saint Kitts and	Trinidad/Tobago
Northern Ireland	Nevis	Thailand
Panama	Saint Lucia	Tibet
Paraguay	Saint Vincent	Turkey
Peru	Serbia (Yugoslavia)	United Kingdom
Pitcairn	Slovenia	United States
Philippines	South Africa	Ukraine
Poland	Sri Lanka	Uruguay
Portugal	Sweden	Vietnam
Romania	Switzerland	
Russia	Taiwan	

Did You Know . . .

. . . regardless of a parent's citizenship status, *any* child born on United States soil is a U.S. citizen.

Embassies in the United States

If you have questions concerning dual citizenship, your visa, or concerns with the naturalization process that you would like answered by someone with specific knowledge about your home country, contact that embassy here in the United States. There is a list of embassies in the United States in Appendix A.

In Conclusion . . .

As you can see, and may encounter as you progress through the process, there are many exceptions to the rules and special situations in the naturalization process. Some of these may pertain to you and some of these may not. Either way, it is important for you to know that they exist so that you can decide what they mean to you. At *any* point during the process, if you are confused and unsure if an exception applies to you, seek professional help; contact your embassy, legal counsel, or the USCIS.

☆ ☆ ☆
CARLA'S STORY

BECOMING A Citizen of the World: A note for U.S. parents of foreign-born children

Congratulations on your new baby! Soon after the initial excitement subsides, new parents abroad have to start dealing with an overwhelming amount of red tape related to establishing a child's official identity and claim to a land. C'est what? Yes, this can be a complicated process with which new parents have to contend. Many children born in the past decade have parents of different nationalities, or have been born as expatriates—outside of the United States. Our daughters had a double whammy: born to expats living in Europe, with the added bonus of having non-European parents (American mother, Canadian father). In the virtual world of technology, geography and physical presence become irrelevant, but not in the realm of government bureaucracy. Nowhere is it more obvious that policies have not kept pace with the realities of globalization and international mobility, than in the matter of dual nationalities.

To provide you with every detail surrounding newborn citizenships for each country is virtually impossible, and quite likely to change by the time your little citizen of the world is faced with the need for a passport photo. Keep in mind though that the policy and the process are two different things; and, the policies are often not reciprocal and usually conflict. Below, I've outlined the policies of the countries that were relevant to us to give you an idea of the process and some helpful hints based on one mom's experience.

No matter where you find yourself when your baby is born, you can count on numerous steps to establish his or her identity—registering of a newborn, obtaining his or her passport, and acquiring residency permits and social insurance numbers. With all of these steps come piles of documents, paperwork, and stress! Nothing is simple, because official and unofficial policies coexist. What's written on paper and communicated by phone or in person usually differ when it comes to establishing newborn citizenship. There seems to be lots of room for interpretation in many personal cases. How many of you know people who hold multiple passports, but their respective home countries don't officially allow it?

☆ RECIPROCAL: interchangeable; complementary

UNITED STATES

Excerpts from the written policy of the U.S. Embassy in Canada read: "... When a person is naturalized in a foreign state (or otherwise possesses another nationality) and is thereafter found not to have lost U.S. citizenship, the individual consequently may possess dual nationality. It is prudent, however, to check with authorities of the other country to see if dual nationality is permissible under local law. The United States does not favor dual nationality as a matter of policy, but does recognize its existence in individual cases." In other words, the U.S. government sort of turns a blind eye to such cases. The government doesn't need to know about dual citizenship unless you wish to relinquish (give up) your U.S. citizenship. Why would anyone want to relinquish his or her U.S. citizenship? One reason for some individuals is because of the disadvantage associated with lifelong tax-filing obligation. Unlike most other countries, tax liability is based on U.S. citizenship and not physical presence. This means that even if you choose to live abroad for the rest of your life as a U.S. citizen, you must continue to pay taxes every year.

The process in the United States is relatively straightforward. It's three-step and hence involves three different applications: Certificate of Birth Abroad, Passport, and Social Security Number. The first two are done on the spot and the last can take up to six months. You need to present your child and swear in front of the consul that all of the statements on your various application forms are true and correct, at least to your knowledge. The part I found funny was that the passport form requires you to indicate personal attributes such as eye and hair color. Aren't most babies initially bald? These things change, yet the passport is valid for five years!

The only tricky part or hassle for some may be proving that you lived in the United States as a citizen for five consecutive years following your 14th birthday. I bet you never thought you'd have to dig out those high school or university records, tax filings, or W-2 forms! Among other reasons, the reason for showing proof of residency is because there's been a recent crackdown due to the rise of child kidnappings. The embassies/consulates abroad follow these rules strictly, so be prepared.

CANADA

The policy resembles that of the United States and the process is also relatively straightforward, but the process takes longer. This passport is valid for ten years. Your child will thus have to live with an embarrassing baby photo for a decade.

GERMANY

My first daughter was born in Germany, but she can claim Canadian and U.S. citizenship through her parents, respectively, although she had never stepped foot in either place. However, she cannot claim German citizenship. This is because German-ness to this day is defined by blood. If you can prove that you are of German descent, then you are entitled to its citizenship. I can't provide much more detail, as this was not the case for my daughter, so the process ended before it started. If your child is a boy, Germany's obligatory military service for all males may be a strong consideration for you. Given that the United States has an all-volunteer military, this is something that one might not have thought about. Rules may change; the French and other European governments have recently done away with their obligatory military service. Your child would likely have the option of revoking his citizenship by the time he turns 18 if he wasn't interested in serving in the army. In any case, you should be aware of the obligations as well as the privileges of holding a particular citizenship.

SPAIN

In Spain, if both parents are non-European, then the child is not permitted to obtain a Spanish passport at the time of birth. However, if the child legally resides in Spain for two years, then the parents can apply for a passport. It is prohibited, though, to possess a passport from more than one country; hence, your child would be required to give up all other passports. Given that my daughter is only a few months old, and we don't actually know how long we'll live here, we'll wait and see what happens. It may be worthwhile to apply for the Spanish passport, knowing that the laws change regularly here. And, we see holding an EU passport as a benefit for future career possibilities, provided we can overcome the obstacles.

Confused? If so, don't worry; you're not alone. Here are some basic practical tips to help you survive the process, no matter what nationalities you will be pursuing for your children:

◆ Keep your official records/files accessible and well organized.
◆ Be mindful about saving original documents like passports, medical and marriage certificates, and other legal records.

◆ Be prepared to take lots of newborn ID photos before you get it right, and once you do, you'll need to provide the proper format and size (this is something that is definitely not standardized across countries!).

◆ Be ready to repeatedly pay money for each little step in each country, such as translation of documents into various languages.

◆ Remain informed of the applicable countries' laws because the myths and realities of dual citizenship are ever-changing.

◆ Be patient.

In closing, have no fear; your baby will have an identity and will belong to at least one nation—eventually—once all the paperwork is done. All of this is a small price to pay in exchange for experiencing the world as a dual citizen. Be assured that once you survive the bureaucratic process, you are giving your child a future advantage both from a personal and professional standpoint. The pros of being bicultural will continue to outweigh the cons as the world becomes more and more interdependent in the twenty-first century. Holding dual nationalities will open up many doors for your child's future, if nothing more than providing him or her with a wonderful international perspective—an asset no matter what land or path he or she chooses. In the end, we can hope and expect that dual nationals will promote better cross-cultural understanding.

Useful Contact Information

USCIS District and Suboffices

The USCIS has a comprehensive website with addresses, phone numbers, and other vital information regarding district offices and suboffices nationwide. To access the site, log on to www.uscis.gov.

You can also call the USCIS toll free at:

1-800-375-5283 or **1-800-767-1833** (TTY)

Here is a state-by-state listing of district and suboffices:
(also available at www.uscis.gov/graphics/fieldoffices/distsub_offices. htm)

ALABAMA
Atlanta, Georgia District Office
Martin Luther King Jr. Federal Building
77 Forsyth Street, SW
Atlanta, GA 30303

ALASKA
Anchorage
620 East 10th Avenue
Suite 10
Anchorage, AL 99501

ARIZONA
Phoenix
2035 North Central Avenue
Phoenix, AZ 85004

Tucson
6431 South Country Club Road
Tucson, AZ 85706-5907
(Suboffice serving Cochise, Pima, Santa
Cruz, Graham, and Pinal.)

ARKANSAS
Fort Smith
4977 Old Greenwood Road
Fort Smith, AR 72903
(Suboffice serving western Arkansas.
The district office is located in New
Orleans.)

CALIFORNIA
Los Angeles
300 North Los Angeles Street
Room 1001
Los Angeles, CA 90012
(District office serving Los Angeles,
Orange, Riverside, San Bernardino,
Santa Barbara, San Luis Obispo, and
Ventura counties. There are also offices
in East Los Angeles, El Monte, Bell,
Bellflower, Westminster, Santa Ana,
Camarillo, Riverside, San Pedro, Los
Angeles International Airport, Lompoc,
and Lancaster.)

San Bernardino
655 West Rialto Avenue
San Bernardino, CA 92410-3327

San Diego
880 Front Street
Suite 1234
San Diego, CA 92101
(District office serving San Diego and
Imperial counties.)

San Francisco
444 Washington Street
San Francisco, CA 94111
(District office serving Alameda, Contra
Costa, Del Norte, Humboldt, Lake,
Marin, Mendocino, Napa, San Francisco,
San Mateo, Sonoma, and Trinity.)

Fresno
1177 Fulton Mall
Fresno, CA 93721-1913
(Suboffice serving Fresno, Inyo, Kern,
Kings, Madera, Mariposa, Merced,
Mono, and Tulare.)

Sacramento
650 Capitol Mall
Sacramento, CA 95814
(Suboffice serving Alpine, Amador, Butte,
Calaveras, Colusa, El Dorado, Glenn,
Lassen, Modoc, Nevada, Placer,
Plumas, Sacramento, San Joaquin,
Shasta, Sierra, Sutter, Siskiyou, Solano,
Tehama, Tuolumne, Yolo, and Yuba.)

San Jose
1887 Monterey Road
San Jose, CA 95112
(Suboffice serving Monterey, San Benito,
Santa Clara, and Santa Cruz.)

Santa Ana
34 Civic Center Plaza
Federal Building
Santa Ana, CA 92701

COLORADO
Denver
4730 Paris Street
Denver, CO 80239

CONNECTICUT
Hartford
450 Main Street
4th Floor
Hartford, CT 06103-3060
(Suboffice serving Connecticut. The district office is located in Boston.)

DELAWARE
Dover
1305 McD Drive
Dover, DE 19901
(Satellite office. District office is in Philadelphia.)

DISTRICT OF COLUMBIA (WASHINGTON, D.C.)
2675 Propensity Avenue
Fairfax, VA 22031
(District office serving the entire state of Virginia and the District of Columbia)

FLORIDA
Miami
7880 Biscayne Boulevard
Miami, FL 33138
(District office)

Jacksonville
4121 Southpoint Boulevard
Jacksonville, FL 32216
(Suboffice serving Alachua, Baker, Bay, Bradford, Calhoun, Clay, Columbia, Dixie, Duval, Escambia, Franklin, Gadsden, Gilchrist, Gulf, Hamilton, Holmes, Jackson, Jefferson, Lafayette, Leon, Levy, Liberty, Madison, Nassau, Okaloosa, Putnam, Santa Rosa, St. Johns, Suwanee, Taylor, Union, Wakulla, Walton, and Washington.)

Orlando
9403 Tradeport Drive
Orlando, FL 32827
(Suboffice serving Orange, Osceola, Seminole, Lake, Brevard, Flagler, Volusia, Marion, and Sumter.)

Tampa
5524 West Cypress Street
Tampa, FL 33607-1708
(Suboffice serving Citrus, Hernando, Pasco, Pinellas, Hillsborough, Polk, Hardee, Manatee, Sarasota, De Soto, Charlotte, and Lee.)

West Palm Beach
326 Fern Street,
Suite 200
West Palm Beach, FL 33401
(Suboffice serving Palm Beach, Martin, St. Lucie, Indian River, Okeechobee, Hendry, Glades, and Highland counties.)

GEORGIA
Atlanta
Martin Luther King Jr. Federal Building
77 Forsyth Street, SW
Atlanta, GA 30303

GUAM
Agana
Sirena Plaza
108 Hernan Cortez Avenue
Suite 100
Hagatna, Guam 96910
(Suboffice serving Guam and the Northern Mariana Islands. District office is located in Honolulu.)

HAWAII
Honolulu
595 Ala Moana Boulevard
Honolulu, HI 96813
(District office serving Hawaii, the
   Territory of Guam, and the
   Commonwealth of Northern Marianas.)

IDAHO
Boise
1185 South Vinnell Way
Room 108
Boise, ID 83709
(Suboffice serving southwest and south
   central Idaho. The district office is
   located in Helena, Montana.)

ILLINOIS
Chicago
101 West Congress Parkway
Chicago, IL 60605

INDIANA
Indianapolis
950 North Meridian Street
Room 400
Indianapolis, IN 46204-3915
(Suboffice serving the state of Indiana
   except Lake, Porter, LaPorte, and St.
   Joseph counties in northwest Indiana.
   Residents of those four counties are
   served by the Chicago district office.)

IOWA
Des Moines
210 Walnut Street
Room 369
Federal Building
Des Moines, IA 50309
(Satellite office. The district office is
   located in Omaha, Nebraska.)

KANSAS
Wichita
271 West 3rd Street North
Suite 1050
Wichita, KS 67202-1212
(Satellite office serving western Kansas.
   The district office is located in Kansas
   City, Missouri.)

KENTUCKY
Louisville
USCIS-Louisville
Room 390
601 West Broadway
Louisville, KY 40202
(Suboffice serving Kentucky.)

LOUISIANA
New Orleans
Metairie Centre
2424 Edenbom Avenue
Third Floor (Suite 300)
Metairie, LA 70001
(Serving Louisiana, Arkansas, Tennessee,
   and Kentucky.)

MAINE
Portland
176 Gannett Drive
South Portland, ME 04106
(Serving Maine and Vermont.)

MARYLAND
Baltimore
Fallon Federal Building
31 Hopkins Plaza
Baltimore, MD 21201

MASSACHUSETTS
Boston
John F. Kennedy Federal Building
Government Center
Boston, MA 02203

MICHIGAN
Detroit
333 Mt. Elliott
Detroit, MI 48207

MINNESOTA
St. Paul
2901 Metro Drive
Suite 100
Bloomington, MN 55425
(Serving Minnesota, North Dakota, and South Dakota.)

MISSISSIPPI
New Orleans District Office (see Louisiana)

MISSOURI
Kansas City
9747 Northwest Conant Avenue
Kansas City, MO 64153
(District office serving Missouri and Kansas.)

St. Louis
Robert A. Young Federal Building
1222 Spruce Street
Room 1.100
St. Louis, Missouri 63103-2815
(Suboffice serving eastern part of Missouri.)

MONTANA
Helena
2800 Skyway Drive
Helena, MT 59602
(District office for Montana and portions of Idaho.)

NEBRASKA
Omaha
1717 Avenue H
Omaha, NE 68110-2752
(District office serving Nebraska and Iowa.)

NEVADA
Las Vegas
3373 Pepper Lane
Las Vegas, NV 89120-2739
(Suboffice serving Clark, Esmeralda, Nye, and Lincoln counties. The district office is located in Phoenix, AZ.)

Reno
1351 Corporate Boulevard
Reno, NV 89502
(Suboffice servicing Carson, Churchill, Douglas, Elko, Eureka, Humboldt, Lander, Lyon, Mineral, Pershing, Storey, Washoe, and White Pine counties.)

NEW HAMPSHIRE
Manchester
803 Canal Street
Manchester, NH 03101

NEW JERSEY
Newark
970 Broad Street
Newark, NJ 07102
(District office serving Bergen, Essex, Hudson, Hunterdon, Middlesex, Morris, Passaic, Somerset, Sussex, Union, and Warren counties.)

Cherry Hill
1886 Greentree Road
Cherry Hill, NJ 08003
(Suboffice serving Atlantic, Burlington,
Camden, Cape May, Cumberland,
Gloucester, Mercer, Monmouth, Ocean,
and Salem counties.)

NEW MEXICO
Albuquerque
1720 Randolph Road, SE
Albuquerque, NM 87106
(Suboffice serving northern New Mexico.
The district office is located in El Paso,
Texas.)

NEW YORK
Buffalo
Federal Center
130 Delaware Avenue
Buffalo, NY 14202
(District office serving the state of New
York, with the exception of New York
City and its surrounding counties.)

New York City
26 Federal Plaza
New York, NY 10278
(District office serving the five boroughs
of New York City, Nassau, Suffolk,
Dutchess, Orange, Putnam, Rockland,
Sullivan, Ulster, and Westchester
counties.)

Albany
1086 Troy-Schenectady Road
Latham, New York 12110
(Suboffice serving Albany, Broome,
Chenango, Clinton, Columbia,
Delaware, Essex, Franklin, Fulton,
Greene, Hamilton, Herkimer, Madison,
Montgomery, Oneida, Otsego,
Rensselaer, Saint Lawrence, Saratoga,
Schenectady, Schoharie, Tioga,
Warren, and Washington.)

NORTH CAROLINA
Charlotte
6130 Tyvola Centre Drive
Charlotte, NC 28217
(Suboffice serving North Carolina. The
district office is located in Atlanta.)

NORTH DAKOTA
St. Paul, Minnesota District Office
2901 Metro Drive
Suite 100
Bloomington, MN 55425

OHIO
Cleveland
AJC Federal Building
1240 East Ninth Street
Room 501
Cleveland, OH 44199
(District office serving the northern part
of Ohio.)

Cincinnati
J.W. Peck Federal Building
550 Main Street
Room 4001
Cincinnati, OH 45202
(Suboffice serving the southern part of
Ohio.)

Columbus
Leveque Tower
50 West Broad Street
Suite 306
Columbus, OH 43215

OKLAHOMA
Oklahoma City
4400 SW 44th Street
Suite "A"
Oklahoma City, OK 73119-2800
(Suboffice serving Oklahoma. District
office is located in Dallas.)

OREGON
Portland
511 NW Broadway
Portland, OR 97209
(District office serving Oregon.)

PENNSYLVANIA
Philadelphia
1600 Callowhill Street
Philadelphia, PA 19130
(District office for Pennsylvania,
  Delaware, and West Virginia.)

Pittsburgh
300 Sidney Street
Pittsburgh, PA 15203
(Suboffice serving western Pennsylvania
  and West Virginia.)

PUERTO RICO
San Juan
San Patricio Office Center
7 Tabonuco Street
Suite 100
Guaynabo, PR 00968
(District office serving Puerto Rico and
  the U.S. Virgin Islands.)

RHODE ISLAND
Providence
200 Dyer Street
Providence, RI 02903
(Suboffice serving Rhode Island. The dis-
  trict office is located in Boston.)

SOUTH CAROLINA
Charleston
1 Poston Road
Suite 130
Parkshore Center
Charleston, SC 29407
(Suboffice serving South Carolina. The
  district office is located in Atlanta.)

SOUTH DAKOTA
St. Paul, Minnesota District Office
2901 Metro Drive
Suite 100
Bloomington, MN 55425

TENNESSEE*
Memphis
842 Virginia Pen Cove
Memphis, TN 38122
(Suboffice serving the eastern half of
  Arkansas, the northern half of
  Mississippi, and the state of
  Tennessee. The district office is located
  in New Orleans.)
*(Naturalization cases in Anderson,
  Bedford, Bledsoe, Blount, Bradley,
  Campbell, Carter, Claiborne, Cocke,
  Coffee, Franklin, Grainger, Greene,
  Grundy, Hamblen, Hamilton, Hancock,
  Hawkins, Jefferson, Johnson, Knox,
  Lincoln, Loudon, Marion, McMinn, Meigs,
  Monroe, Moore, Morgan, Polk, Rhea,
  Roane, Scott, Sequatchie, Sevier,
  Sullivan, Unicoi, Union, Van Buren,
  Warren, and Washington counties fall
  under the jurisdiction of the Louisville,
  Kentucky suboffice.)

TEXAS
Dallas
8101 North Stemmons Freeway
Dallas, TX 75247
(District office serving 123 northern
  counties in the state of Texas and all of
  Oklahoma.)

El Paso
1545 Hawkins Boulevard
Suite 167
El Paso, TX 79925
(District office serving West Texas and
  New Mexico.)

Harlingen
1717 Zoy Street
Harlingen, TX 78552
(District office serving Brooks, Cameron, Hidalgo, Kennedy, Kleberg, Starr, and Willacy.)

Houston
126 Northpoint
Houston, TX 77060
(District office serving southeastern Texas.)

San Antonio
8940 Fourwinds Drive
San Antonio, TX 78239
(District office serving central and south Texas.)

UTAH
Salt Lake City
5272 South College Drive, #100
Murray, UT 84123
(Suboffice serving Utah. The district office is located in Denver.)

VERMONT
St. Albans
64 Gricebrook Road
St. Albans, VT 05478
(Suboffice serving Vermont and New Hampshire. The district office is located in Portland, Maine.)

U.S. VIRGIN ISLANDS
Charlotte Amalie
8000 Nisky Center
Suite 1A First Floor South
Charlotte Amalie,
St. Thomas, USVI 00802
(Suboffice serving St. Thomas and St. John. The district office is located in San Juan.)

St. Croix
Sunny Isle Shopping Center
Christiansted
St. Croix, USVI 00823
(Suboffice serving St. Croix, U.S. Virgin Islands. The district office is located in San Juan.)

VIRGINIA
Norfolk
5280 Henneman Drive
Norfolk, Virginia 23513
(Suboffice serving southeastern Virginia. The district office is located in Washington, D.C.)

WASHINGTON
Seattle
12500 Tukwila International Boulevard
Seattle WA 98168
(District office serving Washington, and ten northern counties in Idaho.)

Spokane
U.S. Courthouse
920 West Riverside
Room 691
Spokane, WA 99201
(Suboffice serving Adams, Benton, Chelan, Asotin, Columbia, Douglas, Ferry, Garfield, Grant, Lincoln, Okanogan, Pend O'reille, Spokane, Stevens, Walla Walla, and Whitman.)

Yakima
415 North Third Street
Yakima, WA 98901
(Suboffice serving Kittitas, Klickitat, and Yakima.)

WISCONSIN
Milwaukee
310 East Knapp Street
Milwaukee, WI 53202
(Suboffice serving Wisconsin. The district office is located in Chicago.)

International Embassies in the United States

The Republic of Afghanistan
2341 Wyoming Avenue NW
Washington, D.C. 20008
Tel: 202-483-6410
Fax: 202-483-6488
www.embassyofafghanistan.org

The Republic of Albania
2100 S Street NW
Washington, D.C. 20008
Tel: 202-223-4942
Fax: 202-628-7342
www.albaniaembassy.org

The Democratic and Popular Republic of Algeria
2118 Kalorama Road NW
Washington, D.C. 20008
Tel: 202-265-2800
Fax: 202-667-2174
www.algeria-us.org

The Embassy of The Republic of Angola
1615 M Street NW
Suite 900
Washington, D.C. 20036
Tel: 202-785-1156
Fax: 202-785-1258

Embassy of Antigua and Barbuda
3216 New Mexico Avenue NW
Washington, D.C. 20016
Tel: 202-362-5122
Fax: 202-362-5225

The Argentine Republic
1600 New Hampshire Avenue NW
Washington, D.C. 20009
Tel: 202-238-6400
Fax: 202-332-3171
www.embassyofargentina.us

Embassy of the Republic of Armenia
2225 R Street
Washington, D.C. 20008
Tel: 202-319-1976
Fax: 202-319-2982
www.armeniaemb.org

Embassy of Australia
1601 Massachusetts Avenue NW
Washington, D.C. 20036
Tel: 202-797-3000
Fax: 202-797-3168
www.austemb.org

Austrian Press & Information Service
3524 International Court NW
Washington, D.C. 20008-3035
Tel: 202-895-6700
Fax: 202-895-6750
www.austria.org

The Republic of Azerbaijan
927 15th Street NW
Suite 700
Washington, D.C. 20035
Tel: 202-337-3500
Fax: 202-337-5911
www.azembassy.us

The Commonwealth of the Bahamas
2220 Massachusetts Avenue NW
Washington, D.C. 20008
Tel: 202-319-2660
Fax: 202-319-2668

Embassy of the State of Bahrain
3502 International Drive NW
Washington, D.C. 20008
Tel: 202-342-0741
Fax: 202-362-2192
www.bahrainembassy.org

The People's Republic of Bangladesh
3510 International Drive NW
Washington, D.C. 20008
Tel: 202-244-2745
Fax: 202-244-5366
www.bangladoot.org/

Barbados
2144 Wyoming Avenue NW
Washington, D.C. 20008
Tel: 202-939-9200
Fax: 202-332-7467

Embassy of the Republic of Belarus
1619 New Hampshire Avenue NW
Washington, D.C. 20009
Tel: 202-986-1606
Fax: 202-986-1805
www.belarusembassy.org

Embassy of Belgium
3330 Garfield Street NW
Washington, D.C. 20008
Tel: 202-333-6900
Fax: 202-333-3079
www.diplobel.us

Belize
2535 Massachusetts Avenue NW
Washington, D.C. 20008
Tel: 202-332-9636
Fax: 202-332-6888
www.embassyofbelize.org

Embassy of the Republic of Benin
2124 Kalorama Road NW
Washington, D.C. 20008
Tel: 202-232-6656
Fax: 202-265-1996

Bolivia
3014 Massachusetts Avenue NW
Washington, D.C. 20008
Tel: 202-483-4410
Fax: 202-328-3712
www.bolivia-usa.org

Embassy of Bosnia and Herzegovina
2109 E Street NW
Washington, D.C. 20037
Tel: 202-337-1500
Fax: 202-337-1502
www.bosnianembassy.org

Botswana
1531-3 New Hampshire Avenue NW
Washington, D.C. 20036
Tel: 202-244-4990
Fax: 202-244-4164
www.botswanaembassy.org

Brazil
3006 Massachusetts Avenue NW
Washington, D.C. 20008
Tel: 202-238-2700
Fax: 202-238-2827
www.brasilemb.org/

Embassy of Brunei Darussalam
3520 International Court NW
Washington, D.C. 20008
Tel: 202-237-1838
Fax: 202-885-0560
www.bruneiembassy.org

Embassy of Burkina Faso
2340 Massachusetts Avenue NW
Washington, D.C. 20008
Tel: 202-332-5577
Fax: 202-667-1882
www.burkinaembassy-usa.org

The Republic of Bulgaria
1621 22nd Street NW
Washington, D.C. 20008
Tel: 202-387-0174
Fax: 202-234-7973
www.bulgaria-embassy.org

Embassy of the Republic of Burundi
2233 Wisconsin Avenue NW
Suite 212
Washington, D.C. 20007
Tel: 202-342-2574
Fax: 202-342-2578
www.burundiembassy-usa.org

Embassy of the Republic of Cameroon
2349 Massachusetts Avenue NW
Washington, D.C. 20008
Tel: 202-265-8790
Fax: 202-387-3826

Royal Embassy of Camodia
4500 16th Street NW
Washington, D.C. 20011
Tel: 202-726-7742
Fax: 202-726-8381
www.embassyofcambodia.org

Canada
501 Pennsylvania Avenue NW
Washington, D.C. 20001
Tel: 202-682-1740
Fax: 202-682-7726
www.canadianembassy.org

The Republic of Cape Verde
3415 Massachusetts Avenue NW
Washington, D.C. 20007
Tel: 202-965-6820
Fax: 202-965-1207
www.capeverdeusa.org

The Central African Republic
1618 22nd Street NW
Washington, D.C. 20008
Tel: 202-483-7800
Fax: 202-332-9893

The Republic of Chad
2002 R Street NW
Washington, D.C. 20009
Tel: 202-462-4009
Fax: 202-265-1937
www.chadembassy.org

Chile
1732 Massachusetts Avenue NW
Washington, D.C. 20036
Tel: 202-785-1746
Fax: 202-887-5579
www.chile-usa.org

Embassy of the People's Republic of China
2300 Connecticut Avenue NW
Washington, D.C. 20008
Tel: 202-328-2500
Fax: 202-588-0032
www.china-embassy.org

The Embassy of Columbia
2118 Leroy Place NW
Washington, D.C. 20008
Tel: 202-387-8338
Fax: 202-232-8643
www.colombiaemb.net

The Republic of Congo
4891 Colorado Avenue NW
Washington, D.C. 20011
Tel: 202-726-5500
Fax: 202-726-1860
www.embassyofcongo.org

Embassy of the Democratic Republic of Congo
1800 New Hampshire Avenue NW
Washington, D.C. 20009
Tel: 202-234-7690
Fax: 202-234-2609

Embassy of Costa Rica
2114 S Street NW
Washington, D.C. 20008
Tel: 202-234-2945
Fax: 202-265-4795
www.costarica-embassy.org

The Republic of Cote d'Ivoire (Ivory Coast)
2424 Massachusetts Avenue NW
Washington, D.C. 20008
Tel: 202-797-0300

The Embassy of the Republic of Croatia
2343 Massachusetts Avenue NW
Washington, D.C. 20008
Tel: 202-588-5899
Fax: 202-588-8936
www.croatiaemb.org

Cuba Interests Section
2630 and 2639 16th Street NW
Washington, D.C. 20009
Tel: 202-797-8518
Fax: 202-986-7283

The Republic of Cyprus
2211 R Street NW
Washington, D.C. 20008
Tel: 202-462-5772
Fax: 202-483-6710
www.cyprusembassy.net

Embassy of the Czech Republic
3900 Spring of Freedom Street NW
Washington, D.C. 20008
Tel: 202-274-9100
Fax: 202-966-8540
www.mzv.cz/washington

Royal Danish Embassy
3200 Whitehaven Street NW
Washington, D.C. 20008
Tel: 202-234-4300
Fax: 202-328-1470
www.denmarkemb.org

Embassy of the Republic of Djibouti
1156 15th Street NW
Suite 515
Washington, D.C. 20005
Tel: 202-331-0270
Fax: 202-331-0302

The Commonwealth of Dominica
3216 New Mexico Avenue NW
Washington, D.C. 20016
Tel: 202-364-6781
Fax: 202-364-6791

Dominican Republic
1715 22nd Street NW
Washington, D.C. 20008
Tel: 202-332-6280
Fax: 202-265-8057
www.domrep.org

Embassy of East Timor
4201 Connecticut Avenue NW
Suite 504
Washington, D.C. 20008
Tel: 202-966-3202
Fax: 202-966-3205

The Embassy of Ecuador
2535 15th Street NW
Washington, D.C. 20009
Tel: 202-234-7200
Fax: 202-667-3482

The Arab Republic of Egypt
3521 International Court NW
Washington, D.C. 20008
Tel: 202-895-5400
Fax: 202-244-4319
www.egyptembassy.us

El Salvador
2308 California Street NW
Washington, D.C. 20008
Tel: 202-265-9671
www.elsalvador.org

Equatorial Guinea
2020 16th Street NW
Washington, D.C. 20009
Tel: 202-518-5700
Fax: 202-518-5252

Embassy of Eritrea
1708 New Hampshire Avenue NW
Washington, D.C. 20009
Tel: 202-319-1991
Fax: 202-319-1304

Embassy of Estonia
1730 M Street NW
Suite 503
Washington, D.C. 20036
Tel: 202-588-0101
Fax: 202-588-0108
www.estemb.org

Embassy of Ethiopia
3506 International Drive NW
Washington, D.C. 20008
Tel: 202-364-1200
Fax: 202-686-9551
www.ethiopianembassy.org

Embassy of Fiji
2233 Wisconsin Avenue NW
Suite 240
Washington, D.C. 20007
Tel: 202-337-8320
Fax: 202-337-1996

Embassy of Finland
3301 Massachusetts Avenue NW
Washington, D.C. 20008
Tel: 202-298-5800
Fax: 202-298-6030
www.finland.org

Embassy of France
4101 Reservoir Road NW
Washington, D.C. 20007
Tel: 202-944-6000
Fax: 202-944-6072
www.info-france-usa.org

Embassy of the Gabonese Republic
2034 20th Street NW
Suite 200
Washington, D.C. 20009
Tel: 202-797-1000
Fax: 202-332-0668

Embassy of the Gambia
1155 15th Street NW
Suite 1000
Washington, D.C. 20005
Tel: 202-785-1399
Fax: 202-785-1430
www.gambia.com/index.html

The Embassy of the Republic of Georgia
1615 New Hampshire Avenue NW
Suite 300
Washington, D.C. 20009
Tel: 202-387-2390
Fax: 202-393-4537
www.georgiaemb.org

German Embassy
4645 Reservoir Road
Washington, D.C. 20007-1998
Tel: 202-298-4000
Fax: 202-298-4249 or 202-333-2653
www.germany-info.org

Ghana
3512 International Drive NW
Washington, D.C. 20008
Tel: 202 686-4520
Fax: 202-686-4527
www.ghana-embassy.org

Embassy of Greece
2221 Massachusetts Avenue NW
Washington D.C. 20008
Tel: 202-939-1300
Fax: 202-939-1324
www.greekembassy.org

Grenada
1701 New Hampshire Avenue NW
Washington, D.C. 20009
Tel: 202-265-2561
Fax: 202-265-2468
www.grenadaembassyusa.org

Guatemala
2220 R Street NW
Washington, D.C. 20008
Tel: 202-745-4952
Fax: 202-745-1908
www.guatemala-embassy.org

The Republic of Guinea
2112 Leroy Place NW
Washington, D.C. 20008
Tel: 202-986-4300

Guyana
2490 Tracy Place NW
Washington, D.C. 20008
Tel: 202-265-6900
Fax: 202-232-1297

The Republic of Haiti
2311 Massachusetts Avenue NW
Washington, D.C. 20008
Tel: 202-332-4090
Fax: 202-745-7215
www.haiti.org

The Holy See (Apostolic Nunciature)
3339 Massachusetts Avenue NW
Washington, D.C. 20008
Tel: 202-333-7121

Honduras
3007 Tilden Street NW
Suite 4M
Washington, D.C. 20008
Tel: 202-966-7702
Fax: 202-966-9751
www.hondurasemb.org

The Embassy of the Republic of Hungary
3910 Shoemaker Street NW
Washington, D.C. 20008
Tel: 202-362-6730
Fax: 202-966-8135
www.huembwas.org

Embassy of Iceland
1156 15th Street NW
Suite 1200
Washington, D.C. 20005-1704
Tel: 202-265-6653
Fax: 202-265-6656
www.iceland.org

Embassy of India
2107 Massachusetts Avenue NW
Washington, D.C. 20008
Tel: 202-939-7000
Fax: 202-265-4351
www.indianembassy.org

The Republic of Indonesia
2020 Massachusetts Avenue NW
Washington, D.C. 20036
Tel: 202-775-5200
Fax: 202-775-5365
wwwembassyofindonesia.org

Iranian Interests Section
2209 Wisconsin Avenue NW
Washington, D.C. 20007
Tel: 202-965-4990
Fax: 202-965-1073
www.daftar.org/Eng/default.asp?lang=eng

Embassy of Iraq
1801 P Street NW
Washington, D.C. 20036
Tel: 202-483-7500
Fax: 202-462-5066
www.iraqembassy.org

Ireland
2234 Massachusetts Avenue NW
Washington, D.C. 20008
Tel: 202-462-3939
Fax: 202-232-5993
www.irelandemb.org

Embassy of Israel
3514 International Drive NW
Washington, D.C. 20008
Tel: 202-364-5500
Fax: 202-364-5428
www.israelemb.org

Embassy of Italy
3000 Whitehaven Street NW
Washington, D.C. 20008
Tel: 202-612-4400
Fax: 202-518-2154
www.italyemb.org

Jamaica
1520 New Hampshire Avenue NW
Washington, D.C. 20036
Tel: 202-452-0660
Fax: 202-452-0081
www.emjamusa.org

The Embassy of Japan
2520 Massachusetts Avenue NW
Washington, D.C. 20008
Tel: 202-238-6700
Fax: 202-328-2187
www.embjapan.org

**Embassy of the Hashemite Kingdom
of Jordan**
3504 International Drive NW
Washington, D.C. 20008
Tel: 202-966-2664
Fax: 202-966-3110
www.jordanembassyus.org

The Republic of Kazakhstan
1401 16th Street NW
Washington, D.C. 20036
Tel: 202-232-5488
Fax: 202-232-5845
www.kazakhembus.org

Embassy of Kenya
2249 R Street NW
Washington, D.C. 20008
Tel: 202-387-6101
Fax: 202-462-3829
www.kenyaembassy.com

The Republic of Korea
2450 Massachusetts Avenue NW
Washington, D.C. 20008
Tel: 202-939-5600
Fax: 202-797-0595
www.koreaembassyusa.org

The State of Kuwait
2940 Tilden Street NW
Washington, D.C. 20008
Tel: 202-966-0702
Fax: 202-364-2868

The Kyrgyz Republic
2360 Massachusetts Avenue NW
Washington, D.C. 20007
Tel: 202-338-5141
Fax: 202-395-7550
www.kgembassy.org

The Lao People's Democratic Republic
2222 S Street NW
Washington, D.C. 20008
Tel: 202-332-6416
Fax: 202-332-4923
www.laoembassy.com

Latvia
4325 17th Street NW
Washington, D.C. 20011
Tel: 202-726-8213
Fax: 202-726-6785
www.latvia-usa.org

Lebanon
2560 28th Street NW
Washington, D.C. 20008
Tel: 202-939-6300
Fax: 202-939-6324
www.lebanonembassyus.org

Embassy of Lesotho
2511 Massachusetts Avenue NW
Washington, D.C. 20008
Tel: 202-797-5533
Fax: 202-234-6815

The Republic of Liberia
5201 16th Street NW
Washington, D.C. 20011
Tel: 202-723-0437
Fax: 202-723-0436
www.embassyofliberia.org

Embassy of Liechtenstein
888 17th Street NW
Suite 1250
Washington, D.C. 20006
Tel: 202-331-0590
Fax: 202-331-3221
http://www.liechtenstein.li/en/fl-aussenstelle-washington-home

The Embassy of Lithuania
2622 16th Street NW
Washington, D.C. 20009-4202
Tel: 202-234-5860
Fax: 202-328-0466
www.ltembassyus.org

Luxembourg
2200 Massachusetts Avenue NW
Washington, D.C. 20008
Tel: 202-265-4171
Fax: 202-328-8270

Embassy of the Republic of Macedonia
1101 30th Street NW
Suite 302
Washington, D.C. 20007
Tel: 202-337-3063
Fax: 202-337-3093
www.macedonianembassy.org

Embassy of Madagascar
2374 Massachusetts Avenue NW
Washington, D.C. 20008
Tel: 202-265-5525
www.embassy.org/madagascar

Embassy of Malawi
2408 Massachusetts Avenue NW
Washington, D.C. 20008
Tel: 202-797-1007

Malaysia
3516 International Court NW
Washington, D.C. 20008
Tel: 202-572-9700
Fax: 202-483-7661

The Republic of Mali
2130 R Street NW
Washington, D.C. 20008
Tel: 202-332-2249
Fax: 202-332-6603
www.maliembassy-usa.org

Malta
2017 Connecticut Avenue NW
Washington, D.C. 20008
Tel: 202-462-3611
Fax: 202-387-5470
http://malta.usembassy.gov

Embassy of the Republic of the Marshall Islands
2433 Massachusetts Avenue NW
Washington, D.C. 20008
Tel: 202-234-5414
Fax: 202-232-3236
www.rmiembassyus.org

The Islamic Republic of Mauritania
2129 Leroy Place NW
Washington, D.C. 20008
Tel: 202-232-5700
Fax: 202-319-2623
http://mauritania-usa.org

Mexico
1911 Pennsylvania Avenue NW
Washington, D.C. 20006
Tel: 202-728-1600
Fax: 202-728-1698
www.embassyofmexico.org

The Federated States of Micronesia
1725 N Street NW
Washington, D.C. 20036
Tel: 202-223-4383
Fax: 202-223-4391

The Republic of Moldova
2101 S Street NW
Washington, D.C. 20008
Tel: 202-667-1130/31/37
Fax: 202-667-1204
www.embassyrm.org

Mongolia
2833 M Street NW
Washington, D.C. 20007
Tel: 202-333-7117
Fax: 202-298-9227
www.mongolianembassy.com

The Kingdom of Morocco
1601 21st Street NW
Washington, D.C. 20009
Tel: 202-462-7979
Fax: 202-265-0161

The Republic of Mozambique
1990 M Street NW
Suite 570
Washington, D.C. 20036
Tel: 202-293-7146
Fax: 202-835-0245
www.embamoc-usa.org

Embassy of the Union of Myanmar
2300 S Street NW
Washington, D.C. 20008
Tel: 202-332-9044
Fax: 202-332-9046
www.mewashingtondc.com

Embassy of the Republic of Namibia
1605 New Hampshire Avenue NW
Washington, D.C. 20009
Tel: 202-986-0540
Fax: 202-986-0443
www.namibianembassyusa.org

Royal Nepalese Embassy
2131 Leroy Place NW
Washington, D.C. 20008
Tel: 202-667-4550
Fax: 202-667-5534

Royal Netherlands Embassy
4200 Linnean Avenue NW
Washington, D.C. 20008
Tel: 202-244-5300
Fax: 202-362-3430
www.netherlands-embassy.org

New Zealand Embassy
37 Observatory Circle
Washington, D.C. 20008
Tel: 202-328-4800
Fax: 202-667-5227
www.nzemb.org

The Republic of Nicaragua
1627 New Hampshire Avenue NW
Washington, D.C. 20009
Tel: 202-939-6570
Fax: 202-939-6542

The Republic of Niger
2204 R Street NW
Washington, D.C. 20008
Tel: 202-483-4224
Fax: 202-483-3169
www.nigerembassyusa.org

The Federal Republic of Nigeria
1333 16th Street NW
Washington, D.C. 20036
Tel: 202-986-8400
Fax: 202-462-7124
www.nigeriaembassyusa.org

Royal Norwegian Embassy
2720 34th Street NW
Washington, D.C. 20008
Tel: 202-333-6000
Fax: 202-337-0870
www.norway.org

The Sultanate of Oman
2535 Belmont Road NW
Washington, D.C. 20008
Tel: 202-387-1980
Fax: 202-745-4933

The Islamic Republic of Pakistan
3517 International Court
Washington, D.C. 20008
Tel: 202-243-6500
Fax: 202-686-1534
www.embassyofpakistan.com

The Republic of Panama
2862 McGill Terrace NW
Washington, D.C. 20008
Tel: 202-483-1407
Fax: 202-483-8413
www.embassyofpanama.com

Embassy of Papua New Guinea
1779 Massachusetts Avenue NW
Suite 805
Washington, D.C. 20036
Tel: 202-745-3680
Fax: 202-745-3679
www.pngembassy.org

Paraguay
2400 Massachusetts Avenue NW
Washington, D.C. 20008
Tel: 202-483-6960
Fax: 202-234-4508

Embassy of Peru
1700 Massachusetts Avenue NW
Washington, D.C. 20036
Tel: 202-833-9860
Fax: 202-659-8124
www.peruvianembassy.us

Embassy of the Philippines
1600 Massachusetts Avenue NW
Washington, D.C. 20036
Tel: 202-467-9300
Fax: 202-467-9417
www.philippineembassy-usa.org

Embassy of Poland
2640 16th Street NW
Washington, D.C. 20009
Tel: 202-234-3800
Fax: 202-328-6271
www.polandembassy.org

Embassy of Portugal
2125 Kalorama Road NW
Washington, D.C. 20008
Tel: 202-328-8610
Fax: 202-462-3726
www.portugalemb.org

Embassy of The State of Qatar
2555 M Street NW
Washington, D.C. 20037
Tel: 202-274-1600
Fax: 202-237-0061
www.qatarembassy.net

Embassy of Romania
1607 23rd Street NW
Washington, D.C. 20008
Tel: 202-332-4848
Fax: 202-232-4748
www.roembus.org

Embassy of the Russian Federation
2650 Wisconsin Avenue NW
Washington, D.C. 20007
Tel: 202-298-5700
Fax: 202-298-5735
www.russianembassy.org

The Republic of Rwanda
1714 New Hampshire Avenue NW
Washington, D.C. 20009
Tel: 202-232-2882
Fax: 202-232-4544
www.rwandemb.org

Embassy of Saint Kitts and Nevis
3216 New Mexico Avenue NW
Washington, D.C. 20016
Tel: 202-686-2636
Fax: 202-686-5740

Embassy of Saint Lucia
3216 New Mexico Avenue NW
Washington, D.C. 20016
Tel: 202-364-6792 /93 /94 /95
Fax: 202-364-6723

Embassy of Saint Vincent and the Grenadines
3216 New Mexico Avenue NW
Washington, D.C. 20016
Tel: 202-364-6730
Fax: 202-364-6736

Royal Embassy of Saudi Arabia
601 New Hampshire Avenue NW
Washington, D.C. 20037
Tel: 202-342-3800
www.saudiembassy.net

Embassy of the Republic of Senegal
2112 Wyoming Avenue NW
Washington, D.C. 20008
Tel: 202-234-0540
Fax: 202-332-6315
www.senegalembassy-us.org

Embassy of Serbia and Montenegro
2134 Kalorama Road NW
Washington, D.C. 20008
Tel: 202-332-0333
Fax: 202-332-3933
www.serbiaembusa.org

Embassy of Sierra Leone
1701 19th Street NW
Washington, D.C. 20009
Tel: 202-939-9261
Fax: 202-483-1793

The Republic of Singapore
3501 International Place NW
Washington, D.C. 20008
Tel: 202-537-3100
Fax: 202-537-0876

Embassy of the Slovak Republic
3523 International Court NW
Washington, D.C. 20008
Tel: 202-237-1054
Fax: 202-237-6438
www.slovakembassy-us.org

Embassy of the Republic of Slovenia
1525 New Hampshire Avenue NW
Washington, D.C. 20036
Tel: 202-667-5363
Fax: 202-667-4563
www.mzz.gov.si/index.php?id=6&L=2

South African Embassy
3051 Massachusetts Avenue NW
Washington, D.C. 20008
Tel: 202-232-4400
Fax: 202-265-1607
www.saembassy.org

Embassy of Spain
2375 Pennsylvania Avenue NW
Washington, D.C. 20037
Tel: 202-452-0100
Fax: 202-833-5670
www.mae.es/en/home

Sri Lanka
2148 Wyoming Avenue NW
Washington, D.C. 20008
Tel: 202-483-4025 /26 /27 /28
Fax: 202-232-7181
www.slembassyusa.org

Embassy of the Republic of the Sudan
2210 Massachusetts Avenue NW
Washington, D.C. 20008
Tel: 202-338-8565
Fax: 202-667-2406
www.sudanembassy.org

Embassy of the Republic of Suriname
4301 Connecticut Avenue NW
Suite 460
Washington, D.C. 20008
Tel: 202-244-7488
Fax: 202-244-5878

Embassy of the Kingdom of Swaziland
3400 International Drive NW
Washington, D.C. 20008

Embassy of Sweden
2900 K Street
Washington, D.C. 20007
Tel: 202-467-2600
Fax: 202-467-2656
www.swedenabroad.se

Embassy of Switzerland
2900 Cathedral Avenue NW
Washington, D.C. 20008
Tel: 202-745-7900
Fax: 202-387-2564
www.swissemb.org

The Syrian Arab Republic
2215 Wyoming Avenue NW
Washington, D.C. 20008
Tel: 202-232-6313
Fax: 202-234-9548

The Republic of China on Taiwan
4201 Wisconsin Avenue NW
Washington, D.C. 20016
Tel: 202-895-1800
Fax: 202-966-0825

Embassy of Tajikistan
1005 New Hampshire Avenue NW
Washington, D.C. 20037
Tel: 202-223-6090
Fax: 202-223-6091
www.tjus.org

The United Republic of Tanzania
2139 R Street NW
Washington, D.C. 20008
Tel: 202-939-6125
Fax: 202-797-7408
www.tanzaniaembassy-us.org

Royal Thai Embassy
1024 Wisconsin Avenue NW
Suite 401
Washington, D.C. 20007
Tel: 202-944-3600
Fax: 202-944-3611
www.thaiembdc.org

The Republic of Togo
2208 Massachusetts Avenue NW
Washington, D.C. 20008
Tel: 202-234-4212
Fax: 202-232-3190

The Republic of Trinidad and Tobago
1708 Massachusetts Avenue NW
Washington, D.C. 20036
Tel: 202-467-6490
Fax: 202-785-3130
www.ttembassy.cjb.net

Tunisia
1515 Massachusetts Avenue NW
Washington, D.C. 20005
Tel: 202-862-1850
Fax: 202-862-1858

Embassy of the Republic of Turkey
2525 Massachusetts Avenue NW
Washington, D.C. 20008
Tel: 202-612-6700
Fax: 202-612-6744
www.turkishembassy.org

Embassy of Uganda
5911 16th Street NW
Washington, D.C. 20011
Tel: 202-726-7100
Fax: 202-726-1727
www.ugandaembassy.us

Embassy of Ukraine
3350 M Street NW
Washington, D.C. 20007
Tel: 202-333-0606
Fax: 202-333-0817
www.ukraineinfo.us

The United Arab Emirates
3522 International Court NW
Suite 400
Washington, D.C. 20008
Tel: 202-243-2400
Fax: 202-243-2432

**The United Kingdom of Great Britain
and Northern Ireland**
3100 Massachusetts Avenue NW
Washington, D.C. 20006
Tel: 202-588-6500
Fax: 202-588-7870
www.britainusa.com/embassy

Embassy of Uruguay
1913 I Street NW
Washington D.C. 20006
Tel: 202-331-1313
Fax: 202-331-8142
www.uruwashi.org

Embassy of the Republic of Uzbekistan
1746 Massachusetts Avenue NW
Washington, D.C. 20036
Tel: 202-887-5300
Fax: 202-293-6804
www.uzbekistan.org

The Embassy of Venezuela
1099 30th Street NW
Washington, D.C. 20007
Tel: 202-342-2214
Fax: 202-342-6820
www.embavenez-us.org

The Embassy of Vietnam
1233 20th Street NW
Suite 400
Washington, D.C. 20037
Tel: 202-861-0737
Fax: 202-861-0917
www.vietnamembassy-usa.org

Embassy of the Independent State of Samoa
800 2nd Avenue
Suite 400D
New York, NY 10017
Tel: 212-599-6196
Fax: 212-599-0797

Embassy of Yemen
2319 Wyoming Avenue NW
Washington, D.C. 20037
Tel: 202-965-4760
Fax: 202-337-2017
www.yemenembassy.org

The Republic of Zambia
2419 Massachusetts Avenue NW
Washington, D.C. 20008
Tel: 202-265-9717
Fax: 202-332-0826

The Republic of Zimbabwe
1608 New Hampshire Avenue NW
Washington, D.C. 20009
Tel: 202-332-7100
Fax: 202-483-9326

Community-Based Resources and Organizations

Many local libraries and state governments offer free courses that help qualified candidates through the entire naturalization process, including preparation for the citizenship test given by the USCIS. Check with your local library and government to see what they offer. In addition, there are many national and community-based organizations that assist candidates with everything from exam preparation to legal services for free or low cost. The following is a list of some of these organizations.

Asian-American Community Service Association
11322-F East 21st Street
Tulsa, OK 74129
Tel: 918-234-7431
Fax: 918-234-3148

Ayuda, Inc.
1707 Kalorama Road NW
Washington, D.C. 20009
Tel: 202-387-4848
Fax: 202-387-0324
www.ayudainc.org

American Immigration Lawyers Association
918 F Street NW
Washington, D.C. 20004-1400
Tel: 202-216-2400
Fax: 202-783-7853
www.aila.org

Catholic Charities USA
1731 King Street
Alexandria, VA 22314
Tel: 703-549-1390
Fax: 703-549-1656
www.catholiccharitiesusa.org

Colombian American Service Association (C.A.S.A.)
8500 SW 8 Street
Suite 218
Miami, FL 33144
Tel: 305-448-2272
Fax: 305-448-0178
www.casa-usa.org

Emerald Isle Immigration Center
Queens Office
59-26 Woodside Avenue
Woodside, NY 11377
Tel: 718-478-5502
Fax: 718-446-3727
www.eiic.org

Bronx Office
280 East 236th Street
Woodlawn, NY 10470
Tel: 718-324-3039
Fax: 718-324-7741
www.eiic.org

Ethiopian Community Development Council, Inc.
901 South Highland Street
Arlington, VA 22204
Tel: 703-685-0510
Fax: 703-685-0529
www.ecdcinternational.org

The Hebrew Immigrant Aid Society
333 7th Avenue, 16th Floor
New York, NY 10001-5004
Tel: 212-967-4100
Fax: 212-967-4483
www.hias.org

Indo-American Center
6328 North California Avenue
Chicago, IL 60659
Tel: 773-973-4444
Fax: 773-973-0157
www.indoamerican.org

Korean American Coalition
3727 West 6th Street, Suite 515
Los Angeles, CA 90020
Tel: 213-365-5999
Fax: 213-380-7990
www.kacla.org

League of United Latin American Citizens Foundation (LULAC)
2000 L Street NW
Suite 610
Washington, D.C. 20036
Tel: 202-833-6130
Fax: 202-833-6135
www.lulac.org

Los Angeles Unified School District Division of Adult and Career Education
2333 South Beaudry Avenue
Los Angeles, CA 90017
Tel: 213-241-1000
www.lausd.k12.ca.us

Lutheran Immigration and Refugee Service
National Headquarters
700 Light Street
Baltimore, MD 21230
Tel: 410-230-2700
Fax: 410-230-2890
www.lirs.org

Maryland Office for New Americans (MONA)
Department of Human Resources
311 West Saratoga Street
Baltimore, MD 21201
Tel: 410-767-7514
www.dhr.state.md.us/mona.htm

The Commonwealth of Massachusetts Office for Refugees and Immigrants
1 Ashburton Place
11th Floor
Boston, MA 02108
Tel: 617-573-1600
www.state.ma.us/ori/

New York Association for New Americans, Inc.
17 Battery Place
New York, NY 10004-1102
Tel. 212-425-2900
www.nyana.org

Services, Immigrant Rights, and Education Network (SIREN)
1425 Koll Circle
Suite 103
San Jose, CA 95112
Tel: 408-408-453-3003
Vietnamese Q&A: 408-286-1448
Spanish Info Line: 408-453-3017
www.siren-bayarea.org

St. Anselm's Cross-Cultural Community Center
13091 Galway Street
Garden Grove, CA 92844
Tel: 714-537-0604
Fax: 714-537-7606
www.saintanselmgg.org

Office of Migration & Refugee Services
United States Conference of Catholic Bishops
3211 4th Street NE
Washington, D.C. 20017-1194
Tel: 202-541-3000
www.nccbuscc.org

For more sites, search www.google.com using the following search terms alone or in combination, along with your home state or city: "naturalization assistance, citizenship assistance, naturalization programs, citizenship programs."

Necessary USCIS Forms

The following USCIS forms and their instructions are exact duplicates of some of the applications and petitions you may need to file during the naturalization process. These are not for official use, but they are good for helping to familiarize you with their format, and what you will need to fill in. To obtain the official forms, you can download them, free of charge, at www.uscis.gov, or call the USCIS Customer Service Line at 1-800-375-5283. It is important to note that the USCIS periodically increases the filing fees for many of these documents, so make sure that you are aware of the proper fees before filing your paperwork.

Form N-400	Application for Naturalization
Form N-426	Request for Certification of Military or Naval Service
Form N-600	Application for Certificate of Citizenship
Form I-130	Petition for Alien Relative
Form I-131	Application for Travel Documen
Form I-140	Immigrant Petition for Alien Worker
	(Form is filed on behalf of an alien)
Form I-485	Application to Register Permanent Residence or Adjust Status
Form I-539	Application To Extend/Change Nonimmigrant Status

New Photo Standards

N-400 Applicatie
for Naturalizatie

Department of Homeland Security
U.S Citizenship and Immigration Services

Print clearly or type your answers using CAPITAL letters. Failure to print clearly may delay your application. Use black ink.

Part 1. Your Name. *(The Person Applying for Naturalization)*

Write your USCIS "A"- number here:
A

A. Your current legal name.

Family Name *(Last Name)*

For USCIS Use Only

Bar Code	Date Stamp

Given Name *(First Name)*   Full Middle Name *(If applicable)*

B. Your name **exactly** as it appears on your Permanent Resident Card.

Family Name *(Last Name)*

Remarks

Given Name *(First Name)*   Full Middle Name *(If applicable)*

C. If you have ever used other names, provide them below.

Family Name *(Last Name)*	Given Name *(First Name)*	Middle Name

D. Name change *(optional)*

Please read the Instructions before you decide whether to change your name.

1. Would you like to legally change your name?   ☐ Yes   ☐ No

2. If "Yes," print the new name you would like to use. Do not use initials or abbreviations when writing your new name.

Action Block

Family Name *(Last Name)*

Given Name *(First Name)*   Full Middle Name

Part 2. Information About Your Eligibility. *(Check Only One)*

I am at least 18 years old **AND**

A. ☐ I have been a Lawful Permanent Resident of the United States for at least five years.

B. ☐ I have been a Lawful Permanent Resident of the United States for at least three years, **and** I have been married to and living with the same U.S. citizen for the last three years, **and** my spouse has been a U.S. citizen for the last three years.

C. ☐ I am applying on the basis of qualifying military service.

D. ☐ Other *(Please explain)* _____

t 3. Information About You.

Write your USCIS "A"- number here:
A

U.S. Social Security Number   **B.** Date of Birth *(mm/dd/yyyy)*   **C.** Date You Became a Permanent Resident *(mm/dd/yyyy)*

Country of Birth   **E.** Country of Nationality

e either of your parents U.S. citizens? *(if yes, see Instructions)*   ☐ Yes   ☐ No

hat is your current marital status?   ☐ Single, Never Married   ☐ Married   ☐ Divorced   ☐ Widowed

☐ Marriage Annulled or Other *(Explain)*

e you requesting a waiver of the English and/or U.S. History and Government
quirements based on a disability or impairment and attaching a Form N-648 with   ☐ Yes   ☐ No
ur application?

e you requesting an accommodation to the naturalization process because of a
sability or impairment? *(See Instructions for some examples of accommodations.)*   ☐ Yes   ☐ No

you answered "Yes," check the box below that applies:

☐ I am deaf or hearing impaired and need a sign language interpreter who uses the following language:

☐ I use a wheelchair.

☐ I am blind or sight impaired.

☐ I will need another type of accommodation. Please explain:

t 4. Addresses and Telephone Numbers.

me Address - Street Number and Name *(Do **not** write a P.O. Box in this space)*   Apartment Number

ty   County   State   ZIP Code   Country

are of   Mailing Address - Street Number and Name *(If different from home address)*   Apartment Number

ty   State   ZIP Code   Country

aytime Phone Number *(If any)*   Evening Phone Number *(If any)*   E-mail Address *(If any)*

(   )   (   )

Part 5. Information for Criminal Records Search.

NOTE: The categories below are those required by the FBI. See Instructions for more information.

A. Gender

☐ Male ☐ Female

B. Height

Feet	Inches

C. Weight

Pounds

D. Are you Hispanic or Latino? ☐ Yes ☐ No

E. Race *(Select one or more.)*

☐ White ☐ Asian ☐ Black or African American ☐ American Indian or Alaskan Native ☐ Native Hawaiian or Other Pacific Islander

F. Hair color

☐ Black ☐ Brown ☐ Blonde ☐ Gray ☐ White ☐ Red ☐ Sandy ☐ Bald (No Hair)

G. Eye color

☐ Brown ☐ Blue ☐ Green ☐ Hazel ☐ Gray ☐ Black ☐ Pink ☐ Maroon ☐ Other

Part 6. Information About Your Residence and Employment.

A. Where have you lived during the last five years? Begin with where you live now and then list every place you lived for the last five years. If you need more space, use a separate sheet(s) of paper.

Street Number and Name, Apartment Number, City, State, Zip Code and Country	Dates *(mm/dd/yyyy)*	
	From	To
Current Home Address - Same as Part 4.A		Present

B. Where have you worked (or, if you were a student, what schools did you attend) during the last five years? Include military service. Begin with your current or latest employer and then list every place you have worked or studied for the last five years. If you need more space, use a separate sheet of paper.

Employer or School Name	Employer or School Address *(Street, City and State)*	Dates *(mm/dd/yyyy)*		Your Occupation
		From	To	

Write your USCIS "A"- number here:
A

)w many total days did you spend outside of the United States during the past five years? [　　] days

►w many trips of 24 hours or more have you taken outside of the United States during the past five years? [　　] trips

st below all the trips of 24 hours or more that you have taken outside of the United States since becoming a Lawful rmanent Resident. Begin with your most recent trip. If you need more space, use a separate sheet(s) of paper.

te You Left the Jnited States (mm/dd/yyyy)	Date You Returned to the United States (mm/dd/yyyy)	Did Trip Last Six Months or More?	Countries to Which You Traveled	Total Days Out of the United States
		☐ Yes ☐ No		
		☐ Yes ☐ No		
		☐ Yes ☐ No		
		☐ Yes ☐ No		
		☐ Yes ☐ No		
		☐ Yes ☐ No		
		☐ Yes ☐ No		
		☐ Yes ☐ No		
		☐ Yes ☐ No		
		☐ Yes ☐ No		

8. Information About Your Marital History.

)w many times have you been married (including annulled marriages)? [　　] If you have **never** been married, go to Part 9.

you are now married, give the following information about your spouse:

Spouse's Family Name *(Last Name)*　　　Given Name *(First Name)*　　　Full Middle Name *(If applicable)*

)ate of Birth *(mm/dd/yyyy)*　　　**3.** Date of Marriage *(mm/dd/yyyy)*　　　**4.** Spouse's U.S. Social Security #

Iome Address - Street Number and Name　　　Apartment Number

y　　　State　　　Zip Code

C. Is your spouse a U.S. citizen? ☐ Yes ☐ No

D. If your spouse is a U.S. citizen, give the following information:

   1. When did your spouse become a U.S. citizen? ☐ At Birth ☐ Other

     If "Other," give the following information:

   2. Date your spouse became a U.S. citizen   **3.** Place your spouse became a U.S. citizen *(Please see Instructions)*

                                                                  City and State

E. If your spouse is **not** a U.S. citizen, give the following information :

   1. Spouse's Country of Citizenship   **2.** Spouse's USCIS "A"- Number *(If applicable)*

                                                   A

   3. Spouse's Immigration Status

     ☐ Lawful Permanent Resident ☐ Other _____

F. If you were married before, provide the following information about your prior spouse. If you have more than one previous marriage, use a separate sheet(s) of paper to provide the information requested in Questions 1-5 below.

   1. Prior Spouse's Family Name *(Last Name)*   Given Name *(First Name)*   Full Middle Name *(If applicable)*

   2. Prior Spouse's Immigration Status   **3.** Date of Marriage *(mm/dd/yyyy)*   **4.** Date Marriage Ended *(mm/dd/yyy)*

     ☐ U.S. Citizen

     ☐ Lawful Permanent Resident   **5.** How Marriage Ended

     ☐ Other _____   ☐ Divorce ☐ Spouse Died ☐ Other _____

G. How many times has your current spouse been married (including annulled marriages)? ☐

   If your spouse has **ever** been married before, give the following information about **your spouse's** prior marriage.
   If your spouse has more than one previous marriage, use a separate sheet(s) of paper to provide the information requested in Questions 1 - 5 below.

   1. Prior Spouse's Family Name *(Last Name)*   Given Name *(First Name)*   Full Middle Name *(If applicable)*

   2. Prior Spouse's Immigration Status   **3.** Date of Marriage *(mm/dd/yyyy)*   **4.** Date Marriage Ended *(mm/dd/yyy)*

     ☐ U.S. Citizen

     ☐ Lawful Permanent Resident   **5.** How Marriage Ended

     ☐ Other _____   ☐ Divorce ☐ Spouse Died ☐ Other _____

Write your USCIS "A"- number here:
A

How many sons and daughters have you had? For more information on which sons and daughters you should include and how to complete this section, see the Instructions.

Provide the following information about all of your sons and daughters. If you need more space, use a separate sheet(s) of paper.

Full Name of Son or Daughter	Date of Birth (mm/dd/yyyy)	USCIS "A"- number (if child has one)	Country of Birth	Current Address (Street, City, State and Country)
		A		
		A		
		A		
		A		
		A		
		A		
		A		
		A		

Add Children

Go to continuation page

se answer Questions 1 through 14. If you answer "Yes" to any of these questions, include a written explanation with this form. Your en explanation should (1) explain why your answer was "Yes" and (2) provide any additional information that helps to explain your ver.

General Questions.

Have you **ever** claimed to be a U.S. citizen *(in writing or any other way)*? ☐ Yes ☐ No

Have you **ever** registered to vote in any Federal, state or local election in the United States? ☐ Yes ☐ No

Have you **ever** voted in any Federal, state or local election in the United States? ☐ Yes ☐ No

Since becoming a Lawful Permanent Resident, have you **ever** failed to file a required Federal state or local tax return? ☐ Yes ☐ No

Do you owe any Federal, state or local taxes that are overdue? ☐ Yes ☐ No

Do you have any title of nobility in any foreign country? ☐ Yes ☐ No

Have you ever been declared legally incompetent or been confined to a mental institution within the last five years? ☐ Yes ☐ No

B. Affiliations.

8. a Have you **ever** been a member of or associated with any organization, association, fund foundation, party, club, society or similar group in the United States or in any other place?   ☐ Yes ☐ No

b. If you answered "Yes," list the name of each group below. If you need more space, attach the names of the other group(s) on a separate sheet(s) of paper.

Name of Group	Name of Group
1.	6.
2.	7.
3.	8.
4.	9.
5.	10.

9. Have you **ever** been a member of or in any way associated *(either directly or indirectly)* with:

   a. The Communist Party?   ☐ Yes ☐ No

   b. Any other totalitarian party?   ☐ Yes ☐ No

   c. A terrorist organization?   ☐ Yes ☐ No

10. Have you **ever** advocated *(either directly or indirectly)* the overthrow of any government by force or violence?   ☐ Yes ☐ No

11. Have you **ever** persecuted *(either directly or indirectly)* any person because of race, religion, national origin, membership in a particular social group or political opinion?   ☐ Yes ☐ No

12. Between March 23, 1933 and May 8, 1945, did you work for or associate in any way *(either directly or indirectly)* with:

   a. The Nazi government of Germany?   ☐ Yes ☐ No

   b. Any government in any area (1) occupied by, (2) allied with, or (3) established with the help of the Nazi government of Germany?   ☐ Yes ☐ No

   c. Any German, Nazi, or S.S. military unit, paramilitary unit, self-defense unit, vigilante unit, citizen unit, police unit, government agency or office, extermination camp, concentration camp, prisoner of war camp, prison, labor camp or transit camp?   ☐ Yes ☐ No

C. Continuous Residence.

Since becoming a Lawful Permanent Resident of the United States:

13. Have you **ever** called yourself a "nonresident" on a Federal, state or local tax return?   ☐ Yes ☐ No

14. Have you **ever** failed to file a Federal, state or local tax return because you considered yourself to be a "nonresident"?   ☐ Yes ☐ No

ood Moral Character.

ne purposes of this application, you must answer "Yes" to the following questions, if applicable, even if your records were
d or otherwise cleared or if anyone, including a judge, law enforcement officer or attorney, told you that you no longer have a
d.

Have you **ever** committed a crime or offense for which you were **not** arrested?	☐ Yes	☐ No
Have you **ever** been arrested, cited or detained by any law enforcement officer (including USCIS or former INS and military officers) for any reason?	☐ Yes	☐ No
Have you **ever** been charged with committing any crime or offense?	☐ Yes	☐ No
Have you **ever** been convicted of a crime or offense?	☐ Yes	☐ No
Have you **ever** been placed in an alternative sentencing or a rehabilitative program (for example: diversion, deferred prosecution, withheld adjudication, deferred adjudication)?	☐ Yes	☐ No
Have you **ever** received a suspended sentence, been placed on probation or been paroled?	☐ Yes	☐ No
Have you **ever** been in jail or prison?	☐ Yes	☐ No

answered "Yes" to any of Questions 15 through 21, complete the following table. If you need more space, use a separate sheet
paper to give the same information.

/hy were you arrested, cited, etained or charged?	Date arrested, cited, detained or charged? *(mm/dd/yyyy)*	Where were you arrested, cited, detained or charged? *(City, State, Country)*	Outcome or disposition of the arrest, citation, detention or charge *(No charges filed, charges dismissed, jail, probation, etc.)*

er Questions 22 through 33. If you answer "Yes" to any of these questions, attach (1) your written explanation why your answer
Yes" and (2) any additional information or documentation that helps explain your answer.

Have you **ever:**

a. Been a habitual drunkard?	☐ Yes	☐ No
b. Been a prostitute, or procured anyone for prostitution?	☐ Yes	☐ No
c. Sold or smuggled controlled substances, illegal drugs or narcotics?	☐ Yes	☐ No
d. Been married to more than one person at the same time?	☐ Yes	☐ No
e. Helped anyone enter or try to enter the United States illegally?	☐ Yes	☐ No
f. Gambled illegally or received income from illegal gambling?	☐ Yes	☐ No
g. Failed to support your dependents or to pay alimony?	☐ Yes	☐ No
Have you **ever** given false or misleading information to any U.S. government official while applying for any immigration benefit or to prevent deportation, exclusion or removal?	☐ Yes	☐ No
Have you **ever** lied to any U.S. government official to gain entry or admission into the United States?	☐ Yes	☐ No

E. Removal, Exclusion and Deportation Proceedings.

25. Are removal, exclusion, rescission or deportation proceedings pending against you? ☐ Yes ☐ No

26. Have you **ever** been removed, excluded or deported from the United States? ☐ Yes ☐ No

27. Have you **ever** been ordered to be removed, excluded or deported from the United States? ☐ Yes ☐ No

28. Have you **ever** applied for any kind of relief from removal, exclusion or deportation? ☐ Yes ☐ No

F. Military Service.

29. Have you **ever** served in the U.S. Armed Forces? ☐ Yes ☐ No

30. Have you **ever** left the United States to avoid being drafted into the U.S. Armed Forces? ☐ Yes ☐ No

31. Have you **ever** applied for any kind of exemption from military service in the U.S. Armed Forces? ☐ Yes ☐ No

32. Have you **ever** deserted from the U.S. Armed Forces? ☐ Yes ☐ No

G. Selective Service Registration.

33. Are you a male who lived in the United States at any time between your 18th and 26th birthdays in any status except as a lawful nonimmigrant? ☐ Yes ☐ No

    If you answered "NO," go on to question 34.

    If you answered "YES," provide the information below.

    If you answered "YES," but you did not register with the Selective Service System and are still under 26 years of age, you must register before you apply for naturalization, so that you can complete the information below:

    Date Registered (mm/dd/yyyy) [   ]   Selective Service Number [   ]

    If you answered "YES," but you did not register with the Selective Service and you are now 26 years old or older, attach a statement explaining why you did not register.

H. Oath Requirements. *(See Part 14 for the Text of the Oath)*

Answer Questions 34 through 39. If you answer "No" to any of these questions, attach (1) your written explanation why the answer was "No" and (2) any additional information or documentation that helps to explain your answer.

34. Do you support the Constitution and form of government of the United States? ☐ Yes ☐ No

35. Do you understand the full Oath of Allegiance to the United States? ☐ Yes ☐ No

36. Are you willing to take the full Oath of Allegiance to the United States? ☐ Yes ☐ No

37. If the law requires it, are you willing to bear arms on behalf of the United States? ☐ Yes ☐ No

38. If the law requires it, are you willing to perform noncombatant services in the U.S. Armed Forces? ☐ Yes ☐ No

39. If the law requires it, are you willing to perform work of national importance under civilian direction? ☐ Yes ☐ No

Write your USCIS "A"- number here:
A

ify, under penalty of perjury under the laws of the United States of America, that this application, and the evidence submitted with it,
ll true and correct. I authorize the release of any information that the USCIS needs to determine my eligibility for naturalization.

Signature

Date *(mm/dd/yyyy)*

t 12. Signature of Person Who Prepared This Application for You. *(If Applicable)*

are under penalty of perjury that I prepared this application at the request of the above person. The answers provided are based on
mation of which I have personal knowledge and/or were provided to me by the above named person in response to the *exact questions*
ined on this form.

rer's Printed Name

Preparer's Signature

(mm/dd/yyyy)

Preparer's Firm or Organization Name *(If applicable)*

Preparer's Daytime Phone Number

rer's Address - Street Number and Name

City

State

Zip Code

NOTE: Do not complete Parts 13 and 14 until a USCIS Officer instructs you to do so.

t 13. Signature at Interview.

ear (affirm) and certify under penalty of perjury under the laws of the United States of America that I know that the contents of this
ication for naturalization subscribed by me, including corrections numbered 1 through _____ and the evidence submitted by me
bered pages 1 through _____ , are true and correct to the best of my knowledge and belief.

scribed to and sworn to (affirmed) before me

Officer's Printed Name or Stamp

Date *(mm/dd/yyyy)*

lete Signature of Applicant

Officer's Signature

t 14. Oath of Allegiance.

ur application is approved, you will be scheduled for a public oath ceremony at which time you will be required to take the following
of allegiance immediately prior to becoming a naturalized citizen. By signing, you acknowledge your willingness and ability to take
oath:

eby declare, on oath, that I absolutely and entirely renounce and abjure all allegiance and fidelity to any foreign prince, potentate,
, or sovereignty, of whom or which I have heretofore been a subject or citizen;

I will support and defend the Constitution and laws of the United States of America against all enemies, foreign and domestic;

I will bear true faith and allegiance to the same;

I will bear arms on behalf of the United States when required by the law;

I will perform noncombatant service in the Armed Forces of the United States when required by the law;

I will perform work of national importance under civilian direction when required by the law; and

I take this obligation freely, without any mental reservation or purpose of evasion; so help me God.

ed Name of Applicant

Complete Signature of Applicant

OMB No. 1615-0053; Expires 06/3

Department of Homeland Security
U.S. Citizenship and Immigration Services

N-426, Request for Certificati
of Military or Naval Servi

Alien Registration Number	Date of Request

NOTE TO CERTIFYING OFFICER: For use in connection with my application for naturalization, please complete the certification of milita service on **Pages 2, 4, and 6** of this form and furnish it to the office of U.S. Citizenship and Immigration Services (USCIS) shown in the address block below. The information shown below is furnished to help locate and identify my military records. **(Submit in triplicate, that is, all six pages of this form.)**

NOTE TO APPLICANT: Furnish as much information as possible. If you were issued a Report of Separation, DD Form 214, attac copy. Fill in the blanks only on Pages 1, 3 and 5 of this form. Please type or print clearly in black ink. All copies must be legible. Do use pencil. **(Submit in triplicate, that is, all six pages of this form.)**

Name Used During Active Service *(Last, First, Middle)*	U.S. Social Security Number	Date of Birth	Place of Birth

For an effective records search, it is important that ALL periods of service be shown below. (Use blank sheet(s) if more space is nee

Active Service:

Branch of Service *(Show also last organization, if known.)*	Date Entered on Active Duty	Date Released From Active Duty	Check Which		Service Number During This Peri
			Officer	Enlisted	
			☐	☐	
			☐	☐	
			☐	☐	
			☐	☐	

Reserve or National Guard Service: ⟶ If none, check ☐ None

Branch of Service	Check Which		Date Membership Began	Date Membership Ended	Check Which		Service Number During This Peri
	Reserve	N. Guard			Officer	Enlisted	
	☐	☐			☐	☐	
	☐	☐			☐	☐	
	☐	☐			☐	☐	

Are you a Military Retiree or Fleet Reservist? ☐ No ☐ Yes

Signature *(Present Name)*	Present Address *(Number, Street, City, State and Zip Code)*

Instructions to Certifying Officer.

Persons who are serving or have served honorably under specified conditions in the armed forces of the United States, inclusive of the rese components of the armed forces of the United States, are granted certain exemptions from the general requirements for naturalization. The requires such service to be established by a duly authenticated copy of the records of the executive department having custody of the record service, showing whether the service man or woman served honorably in an active-duty status, reserve-duty status, or both, and whether separation from the service was under honorable conditions. For that purpose, the certified statement on **Pages 2, 4 and 6** of this form, execu under the seal of your department, is required and should cover not only the period(s) of service shown above, but any other periods of serv (active, reserve or both) rendered by the service man or woman.

Pages 2, 4 and 6 of this form should be completed, or the information called for furnished by separate letter, and the form and letter returned to office of U. S. Citizenship and Immigration Services at the address in the block immediately below.

U.S. Citizenship and Immigration Services

Return to:
Please type
or print
complete
return
address.
Include zip
code.

Applicant: Do not fill out this page.

Certification of Military or Naval Service.

☐ Name correctly shown on front of form.

☐ Name as shown in records:

Active Service.

Entered Service at	2. On	3. Served to	4. Branch of Service	5. State whether serving honorably. If separated, state whether under honorable conditions. If other than honorable, give full details. Always complete item 11.

Reserve or National Guard Service.

Branch of Service	7. Check Which		8. Began	9. Ended	10. State whether serving honorably. State if Selected Reserve of the Ready Reserve. If separated, state whether under honorable conditions. If other than honorable, give full details. Always complete Item 11.
	Reserve	N. Guard			
	☐	☐			
	☐	☐			

Statement Regarding Alienage. *(Complete this item in ALL cases.)*

☐ Record shows this person **was not** discharged on account of alienage.

☐ Record shows this person **was** discharged on account of alienage. Details: _____

Remarks. Use for continuation of any of the above items. You should also show in the space below any **derogatory information** in your records relating to the person's character, loyalty to the United States, disciplinary actions, convictions or other matters concerning his or her fitness for citizenship.

Lodge Act Enlistee.

omplete this block if subject is a "Lodge Act Enlistee"-64 Stat. 316 (Army). Subsequent to enlistment under the Lodge Act on _____

bject entered _____ at the port of _____
(the United States, American Samoa, Swains Island or the Panama Canal Zone)

rsuant to Military orders on _____ via _____

ERTIFY that the information here given concerning the service of the person named on the face of this form is correct according to the records

the _____

(Name of department or organization)

EAL]   **(Official Signature)** _____

Date _____ , _____   By _____

OMB No. 1615-0053; Expires 06/30

Department of Homeland Security
U.S. Citizenship and Immigration Services

**N-426, Request for Certificatio
of Military or Naval Servi**

Alien Registration Number	Date of Request

NOTE TO CERTIFYING OFFICER: For use in connection with my application for naturalization, please complete the certification of militar
service on **Pages 2, 4, and 6** of this form and furnish it to the office of U.S. Citizenship and Immigration Services (USCIS) shown in the address
block below. The information shown below is furnished to help locate and identify my military records. **(Submit in triplicate, that is, all six
pages of this form.)**
NOTE TO APPLICANT: Furnish as much information as possible. If you were issued a Report of Separation, DD Form 214, attach
copy. Fill in the blanks only on Pages 1, 3 and 5 of this form. Please type or print clearly in black ink. All copies must be legible. Do r
use pencil. (Submit in triplicate, that is, all six pages of this form.)

Name Used During Active Service *(Last, First, Middle)*	U.S. Social Security Number	Date of Birth	Place of Birth

For an effective records search, it is important that ALL periods of service be shown below. (Use blank sheet(s) if more space is need
Active Service:

Branch of Service *(Show also last organization, if known.)*	Date Entered on Active Duty	Date Released From Active Duty	Check Which		Service Number During This Perio
			Officer	Enlisted	
			☐	☐	
			☐	☐	
			☐	☐	
			☐	☐	

Reserve or National Guard Service: ⟶ If none, check ☐ None

Branch of Service	Check Which		Date Membership Began	Date Membership Ended	Check Which		Service Number During This Perio
	Reserve	N. Guard			Officer	Enlisted	
	☐	☐			☐	☐	
	☐	☐			☐	☐	
	☐	☐			☐	☐	

Are you a Military Retiree or Fleet Reservist? ☐ No   ☐ Yes

Signature *(Present Name)*	Present Address *(Number, Street, City, State and Zip Code)*

Instructions to Certifying Officer.

Persons who are serving or have served honorably under specified conditions in the armed forces of the United States, inclusive of the reser
components of the armed forces of the United States, are granted certain exemptions from the general requirements for naturalization. The la
requires such service to be established by a duly authenticated copy of the records of the executive department having custody of the record
service, showing whether the service man or woman served honorably in an active-duty status, reserve-duty status, or both, and whether ea
separation from the service was under honorable conditions. For that purpose, the certified statement on **Pages 2, 4 and 6** of this form, execu
under the seal of your department, is required and should cover not only the period(s) of service shown above, but any other periods of serv
(active, reserve or both) rendered by the service man or woman.

Pages 2, 4 and 6 of this form should be completed, or the information called for furnished by separate letter, and the form and letter returned to
office of U. S. Citizenship and Immigration Services at the address in the block immediately below.

U.S. Citizenship and Immigration Services

Return to:
Please type
or print
complete
return
address.
Include zip
code.

Certification of Military or Naval Service.

☐ Name correctly shown on front of form.

☐ Name as shown in records:

			Active Service.		
Entered Service at	2. On	3. Served to	4. Branch of Service	5. State whether serving honorably. If separated, state whether under honorable conditions. If other than honorable, give full details. Always complete item 11.	

			Reserve or National Guard Service.		
Branch of Service	7. Check Which		8. Began	9. Ended	10. State whether serving honorably. State if Selected Reserve of the Ready Reserve. If separated, state whether under honorable conditions. If other than honorable, give full details. Always complete Item 11.
	Reserve	N. Guard			
	☐	☐			
	☐	☐			

Statement Regarding Alienage. *(Complete this item in ALL cases.)*

☐ Record shows this person **was not** discharged on account of alienage.

☐ Record shows this person **was** discharged on account of alienage. Details: _____

Remarks. Use for continuation of any of the above items. You should also show in the space below any **derogatory information** in your records relating to the person's character, loyalty to the United States, disciplinary actions, convictions or other matters concerning his or her fitness for citizenship.

Lodge Act Enlistee.

mplete this block if subject is a "Lodge Act Enlistee"-64 Stat. 316 (Army). Subsequent to enlistment under the Lodge Act on _____

bject entered _____ at the port of _____
(the United States, American Samoa, Swains Island or the Panama Canal Zone)

rsuant to Military orders on _____ via _____

ERTIFY that the information here given concerning the service of the person named on the face of this form is correct according to the records

he _____

(Name of department or organization)

AL]   **(Official Signature)** _____

Date _____ , _____ By _____

OMB No. 1615-0053; Expires 06/3

Department of Homeland Security
U.S. Citizenship and Immigration Services

N-426, Request for Certificati
of Military or Naval Servi

Alien Registration Nu mber	Date of Request

NOTE TO CERTIFYING OFFICER: For use in connection with my application for naturalization, please complete the certification of milita service on **Pages 2, 4, and 6** of this form and furnish it to the office of U.S. Citizenship and Immigration Services (USCIS) shown in the address block below. The information shown below is furnished to help locate and identify my military records. **(Submit in triplicate, that is, all six pa** of this form.)

NOTE TO APPLICANT: Furnish as much information as possible. If you were issued a Report of Separation, DD Form 214, attac copy. Fill in the blanks only on Pages 1, 3 and 5 of this form. **Please type or print clearly in black ink. All copies must be legible. Do** use pencil. **(Submit in triplicate, that is, all six pages of this form.)**

Name Used During Active Service *(Last, First, Middle)*	U.S. Social Security Number	Date of Birth	Place of Birth

For an effective records search, it is important that ALL periods of service be shown below. (Use blank sheet(s) if more space is need
Active Service:

Branch of Service *(Show also last organization, if known.)*	Date Entered on Active Duty	Date Released From Active Duty	Check Which		Service Number During This Perio
			Officer	Enlisted	
			☐	☐	
			☐	☐	
			☐	☐	
			☐	☐	

Reserve or National Guard Service: → If none, check ☐ None

Branch of Service	Check Which		Date Membership Began	Date Membership Ended	Check Which		Service Number During This Perio
	Reserve	N. Guard			Officer	Enlisted	
	☐	☐			☐	☐	
	☐	☐			☐	☐	
	☐	☐			☐	☐	

Are you a Military Retiree or Fleet Reservist?	☐ No	☐ Yes
Signature *(Present Name)*	Present Address *(Number, Street, City, State and Zip Code)*	

Instructions to Certifying Officer.

Persons who are serving or have served honorably under specified conditions in the armed forces of the United States, inclusive of the rese components of the armed forces of the United States, are granted certain exemptions from the general requirements for naturalization. The requires such service to be established by a duly authenticated copy of the records of the executive department having custody of the record service, showing whether the service man or woman served honorably in an active-duty status, reserve-duty status, or both, and whether e separation from the service was under honorable conditions. For that purpose, the certified statement on **Pages 2, 4, and 6** of this form, execut under the seal of your department, is required and should cover not only the period(s) of service shown above, but any other periods of serv (active, reserve or both) rendered by the service man or woman.

Pages 2 ,4 and 6 of this form should be completed, or the information called for furnished by separate letter, and the form and letter returned to office of U. S. Citizenship and Immigration Services at the address in the block immediately below.

U.S. Citizenship and Immigration Services

◄ **Return to:**
Please type
or print
complete
return
address.
Include zip
code.

Form N-426 (Rev. 06/30/06)Y Pa

Applicant: Do not fill out this page.

Certification of Military or Naval Service.

☐ Name correctly shown on front of form.

☐ Name as shown in records:

Active Service.

Entered Service at	2. On	3. Served to	4. Branch of Service	5. State whether serving honorably. If separated, state whether under honorable conditions. If other than honorable, give full details. Always complete item 11.

Reserve or National Guard Service.

Branch of Service	7. Check Which		8. Began	9. Ended	10. State whether serving honorably. State if Selected Reserve of the Ready Reserve. If separated, state whether under honorable conditions. If other than honorable, give full details. Always complete Item 11.
	Reserve	N. Guard			
	☐	☐			
	☐	☐			

Statement Regarding Alienage. *(Complete this item in ALL cases.)*

☐ Record shows this person **was not** discharged on account of alienage.

☐ Record shows this person **was** discharged on account of alienage. Details: _____

Remarks. Use for continuation of any of the above items. You should also show in the space below any **derogatory information** in your records relating to the person's character, loyalty to the United States, disciplinary actions, convictions or other matters concerning his or her fitness for citizenship.

Lodge Act Enlistee.

Complete this block if subject is a "Lodge Act Enlistee"-64 Stat. 316 (Army). Subsequent to enlistment under the Lodge Act on _____

subject entered _____ at the port of _____

(the United States, American Samoa, Swains Island or the Panama Canal Zone)

pursuant to Military orders on _____ via _____

CERTIFY that the information here given concerning the service of the person named on the face of this form is correct according to the records

the _____

(Name of department or organization)

[SEAL]   **(Official Signature)** _____

Date _____ , _____   By _____

Department of Homeland Security
U.S. Citizenship and Immigration Services

**N-600, Application f█
Certificate of Citizensh█**

Print clearly or type your answers, using CAPITAL letters in black ink. Failure to print clearly may delay processing of your application

Part I. Information About You. *(Provide information about yourself, if you are a person applying for the Certificate of Citizenship. If you are a U.S. citizen parent applying for a Certificate of Citizenship for your minor child, provide information about your child).*

If your child has an "A" Numbe█ write it here:

A [   ]

For USCIS Use Only

A. Current legal name
Family Name *(Last Name)*

[   ]

Given Name *(First Name)*   Full Middle Name *(If applicable)*

[   ]   [   ]

B. Name exactly as it appears on your Permanent Resident Card *(If applicable).*
Family Name *(Last Name)*

[   ]

Given Name *(First Name)*   Full Middle Name *(If applicable)*

[   ]   [   ]

C. Other names used since birth

Family Name *(Last Name)*   Given Name *(First Name)*   Middle Name *(If applicable)*

[   ] [   ] [   ]
[   ] [   ] [   ]

D. U.S. Social Security # *(If applicable)*   **E. Date of Birth** *(mm/dd/yyyy)*

[   ]   [   ]

F. Country of Birth   **G. Country of Prior Nationality**

[   ]   [   ]

H. Gender   **I. Height**

☐ Male ☐ Female   [   ]

Returned	Receipt
Date	
Date	
Resubmitted	
Date	
Date	
Reloc Sent	
Date	
Date	
Reloc Rec'd	
Date	
Date	
Remarks	

Part 2. Information About Your Eligibility. *(Check only one).*

A. I am claiming U.S. citizenship through:

☐ A U.S. citizen father or a U.S. citizen mother.

☐ Both U.S. citizen parents.

☐ A U.S. citizen adoptive parent(s).

☐ An alien parent(s) who naturalized.

B. ☐ I am a U.S. citizen parent applying for a certificate of citizenship on behalf of my minor (under 18 years) BIOLOGICAL child.

C. ☐ I am a U.S. citizen parent applying for a certificate of citizenship on behalf of my minor (less than 18 years) ADOPTED child.

D. ☐ **Other** *(Please explain fully)*

Action Block

To Be Completed by
Attorney or Representative, if any.
☐ Fill in box if G-28 is attached to represent the applicant.

ATTY State License #

Home Address - Street Number and Name *(Do not write a P.O. Box in this space)*   Apartment Number

City	County	State/Province	Country	Zip/Postal Code

Mailing Address - Street Number and Name *(If different from home address)*   Apartment Number

City	County	State/Province	Country	Zip/Postal Code

Daytime Phone Number *(If any)*   Evening Phone Number *(If any)*   E-Mail Address *(If any)*

(   )   (   )

Marital Status

☐ Single, Never Married   ☐ Married   ☐ Divorced   ☐ Widowed

☐ Marriage Annulled or Other *(Explain)*

Information about entry into the United States and current immigration status

1. I arrived in the following manner:

Port of Entry *(City/State)*   Date of Entry *(mm/dd/yyyy)*   Exact Name Used at Time of Entry:

2. I used the following travel document to enter:

☐ Passport

☐ Passport Number   Country Issuing Passport   Date Passport Issued *(mm/dd/yyyy)*

Other *(Please Specify Name of Document and Dates of Issuance)*

3. I entered as:

☐ An immigrant (lawful permanent resident) using an immigrant visa

☐ A nonimmigrant

☐ A refugee

☐ Other *(Explain)*

4. I obtained lawful permanent resident status through adjustment of status *(If applicable)*:

Date you became a Permanent Resident *(mm/dd/yyyy)*   USCIS (or former INS) Office where granted adjustment of status

Have you previously applied for a certificate of citizenship or U.S. passport?   ☐ No   ☐ Yes *(Attach Explanation)*

Part 3. Additional Information About You. *(Provide additional information about **yourself**, if you are the person applying for the Certificate of Citizenship. If you are a U.S. citizen parent applying for a Certificate of Citizenship for your **minor child**, provide the additional information about your **minor child**).* **Continued.**

G. Were you adopted? ☐ No   ☐ Yes *(Please complete the following information)*:

Date of Adoption *(mm/dd/yyyy)*   Place of Final Adoption *(City/State or Country)*

Date Legal Custody Began *(mm/dd/yyyy)*   Date Physical Custody Began *(mm/dd/yyyy)*

H. Did you have to be re-adopted in the United States?   ☐ No   ☐ Yes *(Please complete the following information)*:

Date of Final Adoption *(mm/dd/yyyy)*   Place of Final Adoption *(City/State)*

Date Legal Custody Began *(mm/dd/yyyy)*   Date Physical Custody Began *(mm/dd/yyyy)*

I.   Were your parents married to each other when you were born (or adopted)?   ☐ No   ☐ Yes

J.   Have you been absent from the United States since you first arrived? *(Only for persons born before October 10, 1952, who are claiming U.S. citizenship at time of birth; otherwise, do not complete this section.)*   ☐ No   ☐ Yes

If yes, complete the following information about all absences, beginning with your most recent trip. If you need more space, use a separate sheet of paper.

Date You Left the United States *(mm/dd/yyyy)*	Date You Returned to the United States *(mm/dd/yyyy)*	Place of Entry Upon Return to the United States

Part 4. Information About U.S. Citizen Father (or Adoptive Father). *(Complete this section if you are claiming citizenship through a U.S. citizen father. If you are a U.S. citizen father applying for a Certificate of Citizenship on behalf of your minor biological or adopted child, provide information about **yourself** below.)*

A. Current legal name of U.S. citizen father.

Family Name *(Last Name)*   Given Name *(First Name)*   Full Middle Name *(If applicable)*

B. Date of Birth *(mm/dd/yyyy)*   **C. Country of Birth**   **D. Country of Nationality**

E. Home Address - Street Number and Name *(If deceased, so state and enter date of death)*   Apartment Number

City   County   State/Province   Country   Zip/Postal Code

t 4. **Information About U.S. Citizen Father (or Adoptive Father).** *(Complete this section if you are claiming enship through a U.S. citizen father. If you are a U.S. citizen father applying for a Certificate of Citizenship on alf of your minor biological or adopted child, provide information about yourself below.)* **Continued.**

U.S. citizen by:

☐ Birth in the United States

☐ Birth abroad to U.S. citizen parent(s)

☐ Acquisition after birth through naturalization of alien parent(s)

☐ Naturalization

Date of Naturalization *(mm/dd/yyyy)*

Place of Naturalization *(Name of Court and City/State or USCIS or Former INS Office Location)*

Certificate of Naturalization Number

Former "A" Number *(If known)*

Has your father ever lost U.S. citizenship or taken any action that would cause loss of U.S. citizenship?

☐ No   ☐ Yes *(Provide full explanation on a separate sheet(s) of paper.)*

Dates of Residence and/or Physical Presence in the United States *(Complete this only if you are an applicant claiming U.S. itizenship at time of birth abroad)*

Provide the dates your U.S. citizen father resided in or was physically present in the United States. If you need more space, use a separate sheet(s) of paper.

From *(mm/dd/yyyy)*	**To** *(mm/dd/yyyy)*

Marital History

. How many times has your U.S. citizen father been married (including annulled marriages)?

. Information about U.S. citizen father's **current spouse:**

Family Name *(Last Name)*

Given Name *(First Name)*

Full Middle Name *(If applicable)*

Date of Birth *(mm/dd/yyyy)*

Country of Birth

Country of Nationality

Home Address - Street Number and Name

Apartment Number

City   County   State or Province   Country   Zip/Postal Code

Date of Marriage *(mm/dd/yyyy)*

Place of Marriage *(City/State or Country)*

Spouse's Immigration Status:

☐ U.S. Citizen   ☐ Lawful Permanent Resident   ☐ Other *(Explain)*

Is your U.S. citizen father's current spouse also your mother?   ☐ No   ☐ Yes

Part 5. Information About Your U.S. Citizen Mother (or Adoptive Mother). *(Complete this section if you are claiming citizenship through a U.S. citizen mother (or adoptive mother). If you are a U.S. citizen mother applying for a Certificate of Citizenship on behalf of your minor biological or adopted child, provide information about **yourself** below.)*

A. Current legal name of U.S. citizen mother.

Family Name *(Last Name)*　　　　　Given Name *(First Name)*　　　　　Full Middle Name *(If applicable)*

B. Date of Birth *(mm/dd/yyyy)*　　**C. Country of Birth**　　**D. Country of Nationality**

E. Home Address - Street Number and Name *(If deceased, so state and enter date of death)*　　　　Apartment Num

City　　　　County　　　　State/Province　　　　Country　　　　Zip/Postal Code

F. U.S. citizen by:

- [ ] Birth in the United States
- [ ] Birth abroad to U.S. citizen parent(s)
- [ ] Acquisition after birth through naturalization of alien parent(s)
- [ ] Naturalization

Date of Naturalization *(mm/dd/yyyy)*　　Place of Naturalization *(Name of Court and City/State or USCIS or Former INS Office Loca*

Certificate of Naturalization Number　　　　Former "A" Number *(If known)*

G. Has your mother ever lost U.S. citizenship or taken any action that would cause loss of U.S. citizenship?

- [ ] No　　　　- [ ] Yes *(Provide full explanation on a separate sheet(s) of paper.)*

H. Dates of Residence and/or Physical Presence in the United States *(Complete this only if you are an applicant claiming U.S. citizenship at time of birth abroad)*

Provide the dates your U.S. citizen father resided in or was physically present in the United States. If you need more space, use a separate sheet(s) of paper.

From *(mm/dd/yyyy)*	To *(mm/dd/yyyy)*

I. Marital History

1. How many times has your U.S. citizen mother been married (including annulled marriages)?

2. Information about U.S. citizen mother's **current spouse:**

Family Name *(Last Name)*　　　　Given Name *(First Name)*　　　　Full Middle Name *(If applicable)*

Date of Birth *(mm/dd/yyyy)*　　　Country of Birth　　　　Country of Nationality

5. Information About Your U.S. Citizen Mother (or Adoptive Mother). *(Complete this section if you are claiming citizenship through a U.S. citizen mother (or adoptive mother). If you are a U.S. citizen mother applying for a Certificate of Citizenship on behalf of your minor biological or adopted child, provide information about **yourself** below).* **Continued.**

Information about U.S. citizen mother's **current spouse**: *(Continued.)*

Home Address - Street Number and Name

Apartment Number

City   County   State or Province   Country   Zip/Postal Code

Date of Marriage *(mm/dd/yyyy)*   Place of Marriage *(City/State or Country)*

Spouse's Immigration Status:

☐ U.S. Citizen   ☐ Lawful Permanent Resident   ☐ Other *(Explain)*

Is your U.S. citizen mother's current spouse also your father?   ☐ No   ☐ Yes

6. Information About Military Service of U. S. Citizen Parent(s). *(Complete this only if you are an applicant claiming U.S. citizenship at time of birth abroad)*

Has your U. S. citizen parent(s) served in the armed forces?   ☐ No   ☐ Yes

If "Yes," which parent?   ☐ U.S. Citizen Father   ☐ U.S. Citizen Mother

Dates of Service. *(If time of service fulfills any of required physical presence, submit evidence of service.)*

From *(mm/dd/yyyy)*   To *(mm/dd/yyyy)*   From *(mm/dd/yyyy)*   To *(mm/dd/yyyy)*

Type of discharge.   ☐ Honorable   ☐ Other than Honorable   ☐ Dishonorable

7. Signature.

I certify, under penalty of perjury under the laws of the United States, that this application and the evidence submitted with it is all true and correct. I authorize the release of any information from my records, or my minor child's records, that U.S. Citizenship and Immigration Services needs to determine eligibility for the benefit I am seeking.

Applicant's Signature   Printed Name   Date *(mm/dd/yyyy)*

8. Signature of Person Preparing This Form, If Other Than Applicant.

I declare that I prepared this application at the request of the above person. The answers provided are based on information of which I have personal knowledge and/or were provided to me by the above-named person in response to the questions contained on this form.

Preparer's Signature   Preparer's Printed Name   Date *(mm/dd/yyyy)*

Name of Business/Organization *(If applicable)*   Preparer's Daytime Phone Number

( )

Preparer's Address - Street Number and Name

County   State   Zip Code

NOTE: Do not complete the following parts unless a USCIS officer instructs you to do so at the interview.

Part 9. Affidavit.

I, the (applicant, parent or legal guardian) _____ do swear or affirm, under penalty of perjury laws of the United States, that I know and understand the contents of this application signed by me, and the attached supplementary pages number (___) to (___) inclusive, that the same are true and correct to the best of my knowledge, and that corrections number (___) to (___) were made by me at my request.

Signature of parent, guardian or applicant

Date *(mm/dd/yyyy)*

Subscribed and sworn or affirmed before me upon examination of the applicant (parent, guardian) on _____ a

Signature of Interviewing Officer

Title

Part 10. Officer Report and Recommendation on Application for Certificate of Citizenship.

On the basis of the documents, records and the testimony of persons examined, and the identification upon personal appearance of the underage beneficiary, I find that all the facts and conclusions set forth under oath in this application are ☐ true and correct; that the applicant did ☐ derive or acquire U.S. citizenship on _____ *(mm/dd/yyyy)*, through *(mark "X" in appropriate section of law or, section of law not reflected, insert applicable section of law in "Other" block):* ☐ **section 301 of the INA** ☐ **section 309 of the I**

☐ **section 320 of the INA** ☐ **section 321 of the INA** ☐ **Other** _____

and that (s)he ☐ *has* ☐ *has not* been expatriated since that time. I recommend that this application be ☐ *granted* ☐ *denied* and that

☐ *A or* ☐ *AA* Certificate of Citizenship be issued in the name of _____

District Adjudication Officer's Name and Title

District Adjudication Officer's Signature

I do ☐ do not ☐ concur in recommendation of the application.

District Director or Officer-in-Charge Signature

Date *(mm/dd/yyyy)*

DO NOT WRITE IN THIS BLOCK - FOR USCIS OFFICE ONLY..

Action Stamp	Fee Stamp

Law/Visa Category
) Spouse - IR-1/CR-1
) Child - IR-2/CR-2
) Parent - IR-5

)(1) Unm. S or D - F1-1
)(2)(A)Spouse - F2-1
)(2)(A) Child - F2-2
)(2)(B) Unm. S or D - F2-4
)(3) Married S or D - F3-1
)(4) Brother/Sister - F4-1

Petition was filed on: _____ (priority date)

- [ ] Personal Interview
- [ ] Pet. [ ] Ben. " A" File Reviewed
- [ ] Field Investigation
- [ ] 203(a)(2)(A) Resolved
- [ ] Previously Forwarded
- [ ] I-485 Filed Simultaneously
- [ ] 204(g) Resolved
- [ ] 203(g) Resolved

ks:

ationship. You are the petitioner. Your relative is the beneficiary.

filing this petition for my:
- [ ] band/Wife [ ] Parent [ ] Brother/Sister [ ] Child

2. Are you related by adoption? [ ] Yes [ ] No

3. Did you gain permanent residence through adoption? [ ] Yes [ ] No

ormation about you.	**C. Information about your relative.**

e (Family name in CAPS) (First) (Middle)

1. Name (Family name in CAPS) (First) (Middle)

ress (Number and Street) (Apt.No.)

2. Address (Number and Street) (Apt. No.)

or City (State/Country) (Zip/Postal Code)

(Town or City) (State/Country) (Zip/Postal Code)

e of Birth (Town or City) (State/Country)

3. Place of Birth (Town or City) (State/Country)

of Birth dd/yyyy)

5. Gender [ ] Male [ ] Female

6. Marital Status [ ] Married [ ] Single [ ] Widowed [ ] Divorced

4. Date of Birth (mm/dd/yyyy)

5. Gender [ ] Male [ ] Female

6. Marital Status [ ] Married [ ] Single [ ] Widowed [ ] Divorced

r Names Used (including maiden name)

7. Other Names Used (including maiden name)

and Place of Present Marriage (if married)

8. Date and Place of Present Marriage (if married)

Social Security Number (if any) **10. Alien Registration Number**

9. U. S. Social Security Number (if any) **10. Alien Registration Number**

e(s) of Prior Husband(s)/Wive(s) **12. Date(s) Marriage(s) Ended**

11. Name(s) of Prior Husband(s)/Wive(s) **12. Date(s) Marriage(s) Ended**

ou are a U.S. citizen, complete the following:
tizenship was acquired through (check one):
Birth in the U.S.
Naturalization. Give certificate number and date and place of issuance.

_____

Parents. Have you obtained a certificate of citizenship in your own name?
[ ] Yes. Give certificate number, date and place of issuance. [ ] No

ou are a lawful permanent resident alien, complete the owing: Date and place of admission for or adjustment to lawful permanent residence and class of admission.

you gain permanent resident status through marriage to a . citizen or lawful permanent resident?
[ ] Yes [ ] No

13. Has your relative ever been in the U.S.? [ ] Yes [ ] No

14. If your relative is currently in the U.S., complete the following:
He or she arrived as a::
(visitor, student, stowaway, without inspection, etc.)

Arrival/Departure Record (I-94) | Date arrived (mm/dd/yyyy)

| | | | ▬ | | | | | | | |

Date authorized stay expired, or will expire, as shown on Form I-94 or I-95

15. Name and address of present employer (if any)

Date this employment began (mm/dd/yyyy)

16. Has your relative ever been under immigration proceedings?
[ ] No [ ] Yes Where _____ When _____
[ ] Removal [ ] Exclusion/Deportation [ ] Recission [ ] Judicial Proceedings

ECEIPT	RESUBMITTED	RELOCATED: Rec'd	Sent	COMPLETED: Appv'd	Denied	Ret'd

C. Information about your alien relative. (Continued.)

17. List husband/wife and all children of your relative.

(Name)	(Relationship)	(Date of Birth)	(Country of Birth)

18. Address in the United States where your relative intends to live.

(Street Address)	(Town or City)	(State)

19. Your relative's address abroad. (Include street, city, province and country)

Phone Number (

20. If your relative's native alphabet is other than Roman letters, write his or her name and foreign address in the native alphabet.

(Name)   Address (Include street, city, province and country):

21. If filing for your husband/wife, give last address at which you lived together. (Include street, city, province, if any, and country):

From: To:
(Month) (Year)   (Month)

22. Complete the information below if your relative is in the United States and will apply for adjustment of status.

Your relative is in the United States and will apply for adjustment of status to that of a lawful permanent resident at USCIS office in:

. If your relative is not eligible for adjustment of status, he or she

_____
(City)   (State)

will apply for a visa abroad at the American consular post in

_____   _____
(City)   (Country)

NOTE: Designation of an American embassy or consulate outside the country of your relative's last residence does not guarantee acceptance for processing by that post. Acceptance is at the discretion of the designated embassy or consulate.

D. Other information.

1. If separate petitions are also being submitted for other relatives, give names of each and relationship.

2. Have you ever before filed a petition for this or any other alien? ☐ Yes ☐ No

If "Yes," give name, place and date of filing and result.

WARNING: USCIS investigates claimed relationships and verifies the validity of documents. USCIS seeks criminal prosecutions v family relationships are falsified to obtain visas.

PENALTIES: By law, you may be imprisoned for not more than five years or fined $250,000, or both, for entering into a marriage for the purpose of evading any provision of the immigration laws. In addition, you may be fined up to $10,000 and imprisoned for u years, or both, for knowingly and willfully falsifying or concealing a material fact or using any false document in submitting this pe

YOUR CERTIFICATION: I certify, under penalty of perjury under the laws of the United States of America, that the foregoing is correct. Furthermore, I authorize the release of any information from my records that U.S. Citizenship and Immigration Services ne determine eligibility for the benefit that I am seeking.

E. Signature of petitioner.

Date   Phone Number (   )

F. Signature of person preparing this form, if other than the petitioner.

I declare that I prepared this document at the request of the person above and that it is based on all information of which I have any kn

Print Name   Signature   Date

Address   G-28 ID or VOLAG Number, if any.

Form I-130 (Rev. 10/26/0

OMB No. 1615-0013; Expires 11/30/07

I-131, Application for Travel Document

DO NOT WRITE IN THIS BLOCK		FOR USCIS USE ONLY (except G-28 block below)

ocument Issued
-] Reentry Permit
-] Refugee Travel Document
-] Single Advance Parole
-] Multiple Advance Parole

Valid to: _____

Reentry Permit or Refugee Travel ocument, mail to:
-] Address in Part 1
-] American embassy/consulate at: _____
-] Overseas DHS office at: _____

Action Block

Receipt

☐ Document Hand Delivered

On _____ By _____

To be completed by Attorney/Representative, if any.
Attorney State License # _____

☐ Check box if G-28 is attached.

rt 1. Information about you. *(Please type or print in black ink.)*

A #	2. Date of Birth *(mm/dd/yyyy)*	3. Class of Admission	4. Gender
			Male ☐ Female ☐

Name *(Family name in capital letters)* (First) (Middle)

Address *(Number and Street)* Apt. #

City	State or Province	Zip/Postal Code	Country

Country of Birth	8. Country of Citizenship	9. Social Security # *(if any.)*

rt 2. Application type *(check one).*

☐ I am a permanent resident or conditional resident of the United States and I am applying for a reentry permit.

☐ I now hold U.S. refugee or asylee status and I am applying for a refugee travel document.

☐ I am a permanent resident as a direct result of refugee or asylee status and I am applying for a refugee travel document.

☐ I am applying for an advance parole document to allow me to return to the United States after temporary foreign travel.

☐ I am outside the United States and I am applying for an advance parole document.

☐ I am applying for an advance parole document for a person who is outside the United States. *If you checked box "f", provide the following information about that person:*

Name *(Family name in capital letters)* (First) (Middle)

Date of Birth *(mm/dd/yyyy)*	3. Country of Birth	4. Country of Citizenship

Address *(Number and Street)* Apt. # Daytime Telephone # *(area/country code)*

City	State or Province	Zip/Postal Code	Country

TIAL RECEIPT _____ RESUBMITTED _____ RELOCATED: Rec'd _____ Sent _____ COMPLETED: Appv'd. _____ Denied _____ Ret'd. _____

Form I-131 (Rev. 10/26/05) Y

Part 3. Processing information.

1. Date of Intended Departure *(mm/dd/yyyy)*

2. Expected Length of Trip

3. Are you, or any person included in this application, now in exclusion, deportation, removal or recission proceedings? ☐ No ☐ Yes *(Name of DHS office)*:

If you are applying for an Advance Parole Document, skip to Part 7.

4. Have you ever before been issued a reentry permit or refugee travel? ☐ No ☐ Yes *(Give the following information for the last document issued to you)*:

Date Issued *(mm/dd/yyyy)*: Disposition *(attached, lost, etc.)*:

5. Where do you want this travel document sent? *(Check one)*

a. ☐ To the U.S. address shown in **Part 1** on the first page of this form.

b. ☐ To an American embassy or consulate at: City: Country:

c. ☐ To a DHS office overseas at: City: Country:

d. If you checked "b" or "c", where should the notice to pick up the travel document be sent?

☐ To the address shown in **Part 2** on the first page of this form.

☐ To the address shown below:

Address *(Number and Street)* Apt. # Daytime Telephone # *(area/country code)*

City State or Province Zip/Postal Code Country

Part 4. Information about your proposed travel.

Purpose of trip. *If you need more room, continue on a seperate sheet(s) of paper.*

List the countries you intend to visit.

Part 5. Complete only if applying for a reentry permit.

Since becoming a permanent resident of the United States (or during the past five years, whichever is less) how much total time have you spent outside the United States?

☐ less than six months ☐ two to three years
☐ six months to one year ☐ three to four years
☐ one to two years ☐ more than four yea[r]

Since you became a permanent resident of the United States, have you ever filed a federal income tax return as a nonresident, or failed to file a federal income tax return because you considered yourself to be a nonresident? *(If "Yes," give details on a separate sheet(s) of paper.)* ☐ Yes ☐ [No]

Part 6. Complete only if applying for a refugee travel document.

1. Country from which you are a refugee or asylee:

If you answer "Yes" to any of the following questions, you must explain on a separate sheet(s) of paper.

2. Do you plan to travel to the above named country? ☐ Yes ☐

3. Since you were accorded refugee/asylee status, have you ever:
a. returned to the above named country? ☐ Yes ☐
b. applied for and/or obtained a national passport, passport renewal or entry permit of that country? ☐ Yes ☐
c. applied for and/or received any benefit from such country (for example, health insurance benefits). ☐ Yes ☐

4. Since you were accorded refugee/asylee status, have you, by any legal procedure or voluntary act:
a. reacquired the nationality of the above named country? ☐ Yes ☐
b. acquired a new nationality? ☐ Yes ☐
c. been granted refugee or asylee status in any other country? ☐ Yes ☐

rt 7. Complete only if applying for advance parole.

a separate sheet(s) of paper, please explain how you qualify for an advance parole document and what circumstances warrant uance of advance parole. Include copies of any documents you wish considered. *(See instructions.)*

For how many trips do you intend to use this document? ☐ One trip ☐ More than one trip

If the person intended to receive an advance parole document is outside the United States, provide the location (city and country) of the American embassy or consulate or the DHS overseas office that you want us to notify.

y

Country

f the travel document will be delivered to an overseas office, where should the notice to pick up the document be sent:

☐ To the address shown in **Part 2** on the first page of this form.

☐ To the address shown below:

Address *(Number and Street)* Apt. # Daytime Telephone # *(area/country code)*

City State or Province Zip/Postal Code Country

rt 8. Signature. *Read the information on penalties in the instructions before completing this section. If you are filing for a reentry permit or refugee travel document, you must be in the United States to file this application.*

rtify, under penalty of perjury under the laws of the United States of America, that this application and the evidence submitted with e all true and correct. I authorize the release of any information from my records that the U.S. Citizenship and Immigration vices needs to determine eligibility for the benefit I am seeking.

ature Date *(mm/dd/yyyy)* Daytime Telephone Number *(with area code)*

ase Note: If you do not completely fill out this form or fail to submit required documents listed in the instructions, you may not ound eligible for the requested document and this application may be denied.

rt 9. Signature of person preparing form, if other than the applicant. *(Sign below.)*

clare that I prepared this application at the request of the applicant and it is based on all information of which I have knowledge.

ature Print or Type Your Name

Name and Address Daytime Telephone Number *(with area code)*

Number *(if any.)* Date *(mm/dd/yyyy)*

OMB No. 1615-0015; Exp. 07/3

Department of Homeland Security
U.S. Citizenship and Immigration Services

I-140, Immigrant Petiti
for Alien Work

START HERE - Please type or print in black ink.	For USCIS Use Only	

Part 1. Information about the person or organization filing this petition. If an individual is filing, use the top name line. Organizations should use the second line.

			For USCIS Use Only	
			Returned	Receipt
Family Name (Last Name)	Given Name (First Name)	Full Middle Name	Date	
Company or Organization Name			Date	
			Resubmitted	
Address: (Street Number and Name)		Suite #	Date	
Attn:			Date	
City	State/Province		Reloc Sent	
Country	Zip/Postal Code		Date	
IRS Tax #	U.S. Social Security # (if any)	E-Mail Address (if any)	Date	
			Reloc Rec'd	

Part 2. Petition type.

This petition is being filed for: *(Check one.)*

a. ☐ An alien of extraordinary ability.

b. ☐ An outstanding professor or researcher.

c. ☐ A multinational executive or manager.

d. ☐ A member of the professions holding an advanced degree or an alien of exceptional ability (who is NOT seeking a National Interest Waiver).

e. ☐ A professional (at a minimum, possessing a bachelor's degree or a foreign degree equivalent to a U.S. bachelor's degree) or a skilled worker (requiring at least two years of specialized training or experience).

f. ☐ (Reserved.)

g. ☐ Any other worker (requiring less than two years of training or experience).

h. ☐ Soviet Scientist.

i. ☐ An alien applying for a National Interest Waiver (who IS a member of the professions holding an advanced degree or an alien of exceptional ability).

Date	
Date	

Classification:
☐ 203(b)(1)(A) Alien of Extraordinary Ability
☐ 203(b)(1)(B) Outstanding Professor or Researcher
☐ 203(b)(1)(C) Multi-National Executive Manager
☐ 203(b)(2) Member of Professions w/Advanced Degree or Exceptional Ability
☐ 203(b)(3)(A)(i) Skilled Worker
☐ 203(b)(3)(A)(ii) Professional
☐ 203(b)(3)(A)(iii) Other Worker

Certification:
☐ National Interest Waiver (NIW)
☐ Schedule A, Group I
☐ Schedule A, Group II

Part 3. Information about the person you are filing for.

Family Name (Last Name)	Given Name (First Name)	Full Middle Name
Address: (Street Number and Name)		Apt. #
C/O: (In Care Of)		
City	State/Province	
Country	Zip/Postal Code	E-Mail Address (if any)
Daytime Phone # (with area/country codes)	Date of Birth (mm/dd/yyyy)	
City/Town/Village of Birth	State/Province of Birth	Country of Birth
Country of Nationality/Citizenship	A # (if any)	U.S. Social Security # (if any)

If in the U.S.	Date of Arrival (mm/dd/yyyy)	I-94 # (Arrival/Departure Document)
	Current Nonimmigrant Status	Date Status Expires (mm/dd/yyyy)

Priority Date	Consulate

Concurrent Filing:

☐ **I-485 filed concurrently.**

Remarks

Action Block

To Be Completed by
Attorney or Representative, if any
☐ Fill in box if G-28 is attached to represent the applicant.

ATTY State License #

Form I-140 (Rev. 04/01/0

4. Processing Information.

Please complete the following for the person named in **Part 3**: *(Check one)*

[ ] Alien will apply for a visa abroad at the American Embassy or Consulate at:

City

Foreign Country

_____

[ ] Alien is in the United States and will apply for adjustment of status to that of lawful permanent resident.

Alien's country of current residence or, if now in the U.S., last permanent residence abroad.

_____

If you provided a U.S. address in **Part 3**, print the person's foreign address:

_____

If the person's native alphabet is other than Roman letters, write the person's foreign name and address in the native alphabet:

_____

Are any other petition(s) or application(s) being filed with this Form I-140?

[ ] No   [ ] Yes-(check all that apply)   [ ] Form I-485   [ ] Form I-765

[ ] Form I-131   [ ] Other - Attach an explanation.

Is the person you are filing for in removal proceedings?   [ ] No   [ ] Yes-Attach an explanation.

Has any immigrant visa petition ever been filed by or on behalf of this person?   [ ] No   [ ] Yes-Attach an explanation.

If you answered yes to any of these questions, please provide the case number, office location, date of decision and disposition of the decision on a separate sheet(s) of paper.

5. Additional information about the petitioner.

Type of petitioner *(Check one.)*

[ ] Employer   [ ] Self   [ ] Other (Explain, e.g., Permanent Resident, U.S. citizen or any other person filing on behalf of the alien.)

_____

If a company, give the following:

Type of Business

Date Established *(mm/dd/yyyy)*

Current Number of Employees

Gross Annual Income

Net Annual Income

NAICS Code

DOL/ETA Case Number

If an individual, give the following:

Occupation

Annual Income

6. Basic information about the proposed employment.

1. Job Title

2. SOC Code

3. Nontechnical Description of Job

4. Address where the person will work if different from address in **Part 1**.

5. Is this a full-time position?   [ ] Yes [ ] No

6. If the answer to **Number 5** is "No," how many hours per week for the position?

7. Is this a permanent position?   [ ] Yes [ ] No

8. Is this a new position?   [ ] Yes [ ] No

9. Wages per week

$ _____

Part 7. Information on spouse and all children of the person for whom you are filing.

List husband/wife and all children related to the individual for whom the petition is being filed. Provide an attachment of additional family members, if needed.

Name *(First/Middle/Last)*	Relationship	Date of Birth *(mm/dd/yyyy)*	Country of Birth

Part 8. Signature. *Read the information on penalties in the instructions before completing this section. If someone helped you prepare petition, he or she must complete **Part 9.***

I certify, under penalty of perjury under the laws of the United States of America, that this petition and the evidence submitted with it are all true correct. I authorize U.S. Citizenship and Immigration Services to release to other government agencies any information from my USCIS (or for INS) records, if USCIS determines that such action is necessary to determine eligibility for the benefit sought.

Petitioner's Signature　　　　**Daytime Phone Number** *(Area/Country Codes)*　　　　**E-Mail Address**

Print Name　　　　**Date** *(mm/dd/yyyy)*

NOTE: *If you do not fully complete this form or fail to submit the required documents listed in the instructions, a final decision on your petition may be delayed or the petition may be denied.*

Part 9. Signature of person preparing form, if other than above. *(Sign below.)*

I declare that I prepared this petition at the request of the above person and it is based on all information of which I have knowledge.

Attorney or Representative: In the event of a Request for Evidence (RFE), may the USCIS contact you by Fax or E-mail? ☐ Yes ☐ N

Signature　　　　**Print Name**　　　　**Date** *(mm/dd/yyyy)*

Firm Name and Address

Daytime Phone Number *(Area/Country Codes)*　**Fax Number** *(Area/Country Codes)*　　　　**E-Mail Address**

rtment of Homeland Security
Citizenship and Immigration Services

I-485, Application to Register
Permanent Residence or Adjust Status

ART HERE - Please type or print in black ink.

t 1.   Information about you.

y Name	Given Name	Middle Name

ress- C/O

t Number	Apt. #
Name	

	Zip Code

of Birth *(mm/dd/yyyy)*	Country of Birth:
	Country of Citizenship/Nationality:

Social Security #	A # *(if any)*

of Last Arrival *(mm/dd/yyyy)*	I-94 #

ent USCIS Status	Expires on *(mm/dd/yyyy)*

For USCIS Use Only

Returned	Receipt
Resubmitted	
Reloc Sent	
Reloc Rec'd	
Applicant Interviewed	

t 2.   Application type. *(Check one.)*

applying for an adjustment to permanent resident status because:

☐ an immigrant petition giving me an immediately available immigrant visa number has been approved. (Attach a copy of the approval notice, or a relative, special immigrant juvenile or special immigrant military visa petition filed with this application that will give you an immediately available visa number, if approved.)

☐ my spouse or parent applied for adjustment of status or was granted lawful permanent residence in an immigrant visa category that allows derivative status for spouses and children.

☐ I entered as a K-1 fiancé(e) of a United States citizen whom I married within 90 days of entry, or I am the K-2 child of such a fiancé(e). (Attach a copy of the fiancé(e) petition approval notice and the marriage certificate).

☐ I was granted asylum or derivative asylum status as the spouse or child of a person granted asylum and am eligible for adjustment.

☐ I am a native or citizen of Cuba admitted or paroled into the United States after January 1, 1959, and thereafter have been physically present in the United States for at least one year.

☐ I am the husband, wife or minor unmarried child of a Cuban described above in (e) and I am residing with that person, and was admitted or paroled into the United States after January 1, 1959, and thereafter have been physically present in the United States for at least one year.

☐ I have continuously resided in the United States since before January 1, 1972.

☐ Other basis of eligibility. Explain. If additional space is needed, use a separate piece of paper.

_____

_____

_____

already a permanent resident and am applying to have the date I was granted permanent nce adjusted to the date I originally arrived in the United States as a nonimmigrant or ee, or as of May 2, 1964, whichever date is later, and: *(Check one)*

☐ I am a native or citizen of Cuba and meet the description in (e) above.

☐ I am the husband, wife or minor unmarried child of a Cuban, and meet the description in (f) above.

Section of Law
- ☐ Sec. 209(b), INA
- ☐ Sec. 13, Act of 9/11/57
- ☐ Sec. 245, INA
- ☐ Sec. 249, INA
- ☐ Sec. 1 Act of 11/2/66
- ☐ Sec. 2 Act of 11/2/66
- ☐ Other

Country Chargeable

Eligibility Under Sec. 245
- ☐ Approved Visa Petition
- ☐ Dependent of Principal Alien
- ☐ Other
- ☐ Special Immigrant

Preference

Action Block

To be Completed by
Attorney or Representative, **if any**
☐ Fill in box if G-28 is attached to represent the applicant.

VOLAG #

ATTY State License #

Part 3. Processing information.

A. City/Town/Village of Birth

Current Occupation

Your Mother's First Name

Your Father's First Name

Give your name exactly as it appears on your Arrival/Departure Record (Form I-94)

Place of Last Entry Into the United States *(City/State)*	In what status did you last enter? *(Visitor, student, exchange alien, crewman, temporary worker, without inspection, etc.)*
Were you inspected by a U.S. Immigration Officer? ☐ Yes ☐ No	
Nonimmigrant Visa Number	Consulate Where Visa Was Issued
Date Visa Was Issued (mm/dd/yyyy) Gender: ☐ Male ☐ Female	Marital Status: ☐ Married ☐ Single ☐ Divorced ☐ Wid☐

Have you ever before applied for permanent resident status in the U.S.?   ☐ No   ☐ Yes. If you checked "Yes," give date and place of filing and final disposition.

B. List your present husband/wife, all of your sons and daughters (If you have none, write "none." If additional space is needed, use separate paper

Family Name	Given Name	Middle Initial	Date of Birth *(mm/dd/yyyy)*
Country of Birth	Relationship	A #	Applying with you? ☐ Yes ☐ No
Family Name	Given Name	Middle Initial	Date of Birth *(mm/dd/yyyy)*
Country of Birth	Relationship	A #	Applying with you? ☐ Yes ☐ No
Family Name	Given Name	Middle Initial	Date of Birth *(mm/dd/yyyy)*
Country of Birth	Relationship	A #	Applying with you? ☐ Yes ☐ No
Family Name	Given Name	Middle Initial	Date of Birth *(mm/dd/yyyy)*
Country of Birth	Relationship	A #	Applying with you? ☐ Yes ☐ No
Family Name	Given Name	Middle Initial	Date of Birth *(mm/dd/yyyy)*
Country of Birth	Relationship	A #	Applying with you? ☐ Yes ☐ No

C. List your present and past membership in or affiliation with every organization, association, fund, foundation, party, club, society or similar gro in the United States or in other places since your 16th birthday. Include any foreign military service in this part. If none, write "none." Include name(s) of organization(s), location(s), dates of membership, from and to, and the nature of the organization(s). If additional space is needed, us separate piece of paper.

3. Processing information. *(Continued)*

answer the following questions. (If your answer is **"Yes"** on any one of these questions, explain on a separate piece of paper. Answering **"Yes"** ot necessarily mean that you are not entitled to adjust status or register for permanent residence.)

ave you ever, in or outside the United States:

a. knowingly committed any crime of moral turpitude or a drug-related offense for which you have not been arrested? ☐ Yes ☐ No

b. been arrested, cited, charged, indicted, fined or imprisoned for breaking or violating any law or ordinance, excluding traffic violations? ☐ Yes ☐ No

c. been the beneficiary of a pardon, amnesty, rehabilitation decree, other act of clemency or similar action? ☐ Yes ☐ No

d. exercised diplomatic immunity to avoid prosecution for a criminal offense in the United States? ☐ Yes ☐ No

ave you received public assistance in the United States from any source, including the United States government or any state, ☐ Yes ☐ No
ounty, city or municipality (other than emergency medical treatment), or are you likely to receive public assistance in the
ture?

ave you ever:

a. within the past ten years been a prostitute or procured anyone for prostitution, or intend to engage in such activities in the future? ☐ Yes ☐ No

b. engaged in any unlawful commercialized vice, including, but not limited to, illegal gambling? ☐ Yes ☐ No

c. knowingly encouraged, induced, assisted, abetted or aided any alien to try to enter the United States illegally? ☐ Yes ☐ No

d. illicitly trafficked in any controlled substance, or knowingly assisted, abetted or colluded in the illicit trafficking of any controlled substance? ☐ Yes ☐ No

ave you ever engaged in, conspired to engage in, or do you intend to engage in, or have you ever solicited membership or ☐ Yes ☐ No
nds for, or have you through any means ever assisted or provided any type of material support to any person or organization
at has ever engaged or conspired to engage in sabotage, kidnapping, political assassination, hijacking or any other form of
rorist activity?

you intend to engage in the United States in:

a. espionage? ☐ Yes ☐ No

b. any activity a purpose of which is opposition to, or the control or overthrow of, the government of the United States, by force, violence or other unlawful means? ☐ Yes ☐ No

c. any activity to violate or evade any law prohibiting the export from the United States of goods, technology or sensitive information? ☐ Yes ☐ No

ave you ever been a member of, or in any way affiliated with, the Communist Party or any other totalitarian party? ☐ Yes ☐ No

d you, during the period from March 23, 1933 to May 8, 1945, in association with either the Nazi Government of Germany ☐ Yes ☐ No
any organization or government associated or allied with the Nazi Government of Germany, ever order, incite, assist or
nerwise participate in the persecution of any person because of race, religion, national origin or political opinion?

ve you ever engaged in genocide, or otherwise ordered, incited, assisted or otherwise participated in the killing of any ☐ Yes ☐ No
rson because of race, religion, nationality, ethnic origin or political opinion?

ve you ever been deported from the United States, or removed from the United States at government expense, excluded ☐ Yes ☐ No
thin the past year, or are you now in exclusion, deportation, removal or recission proceedings?

e you under a final order of civil penalty for violating section 274C of the Immigration and Nationality Act for use of ☐ Yes ☐ No
udulent documents or have you, by fraud or willful misrepresentation of a material fact, ever sought to procure, or procured,
isa, other documentation, entry into the United States or any immigration benefit?

ve you ever left the United States to avoid being drafted into the U.S. Armed Forces? ☐ Yes ☐ No

ve you ever been a J nonimmigrant exchange visitor who was subject to the two-year foreign residence requirement and ☐ Yes ☐ No
ve not yet complied with that requirement or obtained a waiver?

e you now withholding custody of a U.S. citizen child outside the United States from a person granted custody of the child? ☐ Yes ☐ No

you plan to practice polygamy in the United States? ☐ Yes ☐ No

Part 4. Signature. *(Read the information on penalties in the instructions before completing this section. You must file this application in the United States.)*

YOUR REGISTRATION WITH THE U.S. CITIZENSHIP AND IMMIGRATION SERVICES."I understand and acknowledge under section 262 of the Immigration and Nationality Act (Act), as an alien who has been or will be in the United States for more th days, I am required to register with the U.S. Citizenship and Immigration Services. I understand and acknowledge that, under section of the Act, I am required to provide USCIS with my current address and written notice of any change of address within **ten** days of change. I understand and acknowledge that USCIS will use the most recent address that I provide to USCIS, on any form containing these acknowledgements, for all purposes, including the service of a Notice to Appear should it be necessary for USCIS to initiate removal proceedings against me. I understand and acknowledge that if I change my address without providing written notice to USC will be held responsible for any communications sent to me at the most recent address that I provided to USCIS. I further understand acknowledge that, if removal proceedings are initiated against me and I fail to attend any hearing, including an initial hearing based service of the Notice to Appear at the most recent address that I provided to USCIS or as otherwise provided by law, I may be order removed in my absence, arrested by USCIS and removed from the United States."

SELECTIVE SERVICE REGISTRATION. The following applies to you if you are a male at least 18 years old, but not yet ? years old, who is required to register with the Selective Service System: "I understand that my filing this adjustment of status application with the U.S. Citizenship and Immigration Services authorizes USCIS to provide certain registration information to the Selective Service System in accordance with the Military Selective Service Act. Upon USCIS acceptance of my application, I auth USCIS to transmit to the Selective Service System my name, current address, Social Security Number, date of birth and the date I f the application for the purpose of recording my Selective Service registration as of the filing date. If, however, USCIS does not acc my application, I further understand that, if so required, I am responsible for registering with the Selective Service by other means, provided I have not yet reached age 26."

APPLICANT'S CERTIFICATION. I certify, under penalty of perjury under the laws of the United States of America, that this application and the evidence submitted with it is all true and correct. I authorize the release of any information from my records tha U.S. Citizenship and Immigration Services (USCIS) needs to determine eligibility for the benefit I am seeking.

Signature	*Print Your Name*	*Date*	*Daytime Phone Number*

NOTE: *If you do not completely fill out this form or fail to submit required documents listed in the instructions, you may not be found eligible for requested document and this application may be denied.*

Part 5. Signature of person preparing form, if other than above. (sign below)

I declare that I prepared this application at the request of the above person and it is based on all information of which I have knowledge.

Signature	*Print Your Name*	*Date*	*Daytime Phone Number*

*Firm Name
and Address*

E-mail Address (if any)

rtment of Homeland Security
Citizenship and Immigration Services

I-539, Application to Extend/ Change Nonimmigrant Status

RT HERE - Please type or print in black ink.

	For USCIS Use Only

1. Information about you.

ily Name | Given Name | Middle Name

ress -
are of -

et Number
Name | Apt. #

| State | Zip Code | Daytime Phone #

try of Birth | Country of Citizenship

of Birth
dd/yyyy) | U. S. Social Security # (if any) | A # (if any)

of Last Arrival
the U.S. | I-94 #

ent Nonimmigrant
ls | Expires on
(mm/dd/yyyy)

For USCIS Use Only

Returned | Receipt

Date

Resubmitted

Date

Reloc Sent

Date

Reloc Rec'd

Date

2. Application type. *(See instructions for fee.)*

am applying for: *(Check one.)*
- [ ] An extension of stay in my current status.
- [ ] A change of status. The new status I am requesting is: _____
- [ ] Other: *(Describe grounds of eligibility.)* _____

umber of people included in this application: *(Check one.)*
- [ ] I am the only applicant.
- [ ] Members of my family are filing this application with me.
  The total number of people (including me) in the application is: _____
  (Complete the supplement for each co-applicant.)

- [ ] Applicant
  Interviewed
  on

Date

- [ ] *Extension Granted to (Date):* _____

Change of Status/Extension Granted
New Class: From *(Date):* _____
To *(Date):* _____

3. Processing information.

Ve request that my/our current or requested status be extended until
am/dd/yyyy): _____

s this application based on an extension or change of status already granted to your
pouse, child or parent?
] No [ ] Yes. USCIS Receipt # _____
s this application based on a separate petition or application to give your spouse,
hild or parent an extension or change of status? [ ] No [ ] Yes, filed with this I-539.

] Yes, filed previously and pending with USCIS. Receipt #: _____
you answered "Yes" to Question 3, give the name of the petitioner or applicant:

the petition or application is pending with USCIS, also give the following data:

ffice filed at _____ Filed on (mm/dd/yyyy) _____

If Denied:
- [ ] Still within period of stay
- [ ] S/D to: _____
- [ ] Place under docket control

Remarks:

Action Block

4. Additional information.

r applicant #1, provide passport information: | Valid to: (mm/dd/yyyy)
untry of Issuance

eign Address: Street Number and Name | Apt. #

y or Town | State or Province

untry | Zip/Postal Code

To Be Completed by
Attorney or Representative, if any

- [ ] Fill in box if G-28 is attached to
  represent the applicant.

ATTY State License # _____

Form I-539 (Rev. 04/01/06)Y

Part 4. Additional information.

3. Answer the following questions. If you answer "Yes" to any question, explain on separate sheet of paper.

		Yes	
a.	Are you, or any other person included on the application, an applicant for an immigrant visa?	☐	
b.	Has an immigrant petition ever been filed for you or for any other person included in this application?	☐	
c.	Has a Form I-485, Application to Register Permanent Residence or Adjust Status, ever been filed by you or by any other person included in this application?	☐	
d.	Have you, or any other person included in this application, ever been arrested or convicted of any criminal offense since last entering the U.S.?	☐	
e.	Have you, or any other person included in this application, done anything that violated the terms of the nonimmigrant status you now hold?	☐	
f.	Are you, or any other person included in this application, now in removal proceedings?	☐	
g.	Have you, or any other person included in this application, been employed in the U.S. since last admitted or granted an extension or change of status?	☐	

- If you answered "Yes" to Question 3f, give the following information concerning the removal proceedings on the attached entitled "**Part 4. Additional information. Page for answers to 3f and 3g.**" Include the name of the person in removal proceedings and information on jurisdiction, date proceedings began and status of proceedings.

- If you answered "No" to Question 3g, fully describe how you are supporting yourself on the attached page entitled "**Part** **Additional information. Page for answers to 3f and 3g.**" Include the source, amount and basis for any income.

- If you answered "Yes" to Question 3g, fully describe the employment on the attached page entitled "**Part 4. Additional information. Page for answers to 3f and 3g.**" Include the name of the person employed, name and address of the emp weekly income and whether the employment was specifically authorized by USCIS.

Part 5. Signature. *(Read the information on penalties in the instructions before completing this section. You must file this application while in the United States.)*

I certify, under penalty of perjury under the laws of the United States of America, that this application and the evidence submitted is all true and correct. I authorize the release of any information from my records that U.S. Citizenship and Immigration Services to determine eligibility for the benefit I am seeking.

Signature	Print your Name	Date
Daytime Telephone Number	E-Mail Address	

NOTE: *If you do not completely fill out this form or fail to submit required documents listed in the instructions, you may not be found eligible for requested benefit and this application may be denied.*

Part 6. Signature of person preparing form, if other than above. *(Sign below.)*

I declare that I prepared this application at the request of the above person and it is based on all information of which I have knowl

Signature	Print your Name	Date
Firm Name and Address	Daytime Telephone Number *(Area Code and Number)*	
	Fax Number *(Area Code and Number)*	E-Mail Address

4. Additional information. Page for answers to 3f and 3g.

answered "Yes" to Question 3f in Part 4 on Page 3 of this form, give the following information concerning the removal
:dings. Include the name of the person in removal proceedings and information on jurisdiction, date proceedings began and status
cedings.

answered "No" to Question 3g in Part 4 on Page 3 of this form, fully describe how you are supporting yourself. Include the
:, amount and basis for any income.

answered "Yes" to Question 3g in Part 4 on Page 3 of this form, fully describe the employment. Include the name of the person
yed, name and address of the employer, weekly income and whether the employment was specifically authorized by USCIS.

Supplement -1
Attach to Form I-539 when more than one person is included in the petition or application.
(List each person separately. Do not include the person named in the Form I-539.)

Family Name	Given Name	Middle Name	Date of Birth (mm/dd/yyyy)	
Country of Birth	County of Citizenship	U.S. Social Security # (if any)	A # (if any)	
Date of Arrival (mm/dd/yyyy)		I-94 #		
Current Nonimmigrant Status:		Expires on (mm/dd/yyyy)		
Country Where Passport Issued		Expiration Date (mm/dd/yyyy)		

Family Name	Given Name	Middle Name	Date of Birth (mm/dd/yyyy)	
Country of Birth	Country of Citizenship	U.S. Social Security # (if any)	A # (if any)	
Date of Arrival (mm/dd/yyyy)		I-94 #		
Current Nonimmigrant Status:		Expires on (mm/dd/yyyy)		
Country Where Passport Issued		Expiration Date (mm/dd/yyyy)		

Family Name	Given Name	Middle Name	Date of Birth (mm/dd/yyyy)	
Country of Birth	Country of Citizenship	U.S. Social Security # (if any)	A # (if any)	
Date of Arrival (mm/dd/yyyy)		I-94 #		
Current Nonimmigrant Status:		Expires on (mm/dd/yyyy)		
Country Where Passport Issued		Expiration Date (mm/dd/yyyy)		

Family Name	Given Name	Middle Name	Date of Birth (mm/dd/yyyy)	
Country of Birth	Country of Citizenship	U.S. Social Security # (if any)	A # (if any)	
Date of Arrival (mm/dd/yyyy)		I-94 #		
Current Nonimmigrant Status:		Expires on (mm/dd/yyyy)		
Country Where Passport Issued		Expiration Date (mm/dd/yyyy)		

Family Name	Given Name	Middle Name	Date of Birth (mm/dd/yyyy)	
Country of Birth	Country of Citizenship	U.S. Social Security # (if any)	A # (if any)	
Date of Arrival (mm/dd/yyyy)		I-94 #		
Current Nonimmigrant Status:		Expires on (mm/dd/yyyy)		
Country Where Passport Issued		Expiration Date (mm/dd/yyyy)		

If you need additional space, attach a separate sheet(s) of paper.
Place your name, A #, if any, date of birth, form number and application date at the top of the sheet(s) of paper.

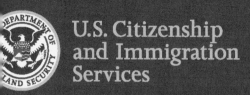

U.S. Citizenship and Immigration Services

**Three-Quarter
e Photo**

**Passport
e Photo**

s Must Be in Color

USCIS Is Making Photos Simpler

Washington, DC — In accordance with language specified in the Border Security Act of 2003, U.S. Citizenship and Immigration Services (USCIS) announced a change in the photo requirements for all applicants from a three-quarter face position to a standard, full-frontal face position to take effect **August 2, 2004**.

USCIS will accept both three-quarter and full-frontal color photographs until **September 1, 2004,** after which only full-frontal color will be accepted.

The application process of customers who have already submitted materials that include color photos with the three-quarter standard **will not** be affected by this change.

All photos must be of just the person. Where more than one photo is required, all photos of the person must be identical. All photos must meet the specifications for full-frontal/passport photos.

For more information on photo standards, visit the Department of State website at http://www.travel.state.gov/passport/pptphotos/index.html, or contact the USCIS National Customer Service Center at 1 800 375 5283.

List of forms that require photos is on the back

M-603 (07/04)

2 photos are required for the following forms:

I-90 – Renew or replace your Permanent Resident Card (green card)

I-131 – Re-entry permit, refugee travel document, or advance parole

I-485 – Adjust status and become a permanent resident while in the U.S.

I-765 – Employment Authorization/Employment Authorization Document (EAD)

I-777 – Replace Northern Mariana Card

I-821 – Temporary Protected Status (TPS) Program

N-300 – Declaration of Intent (to apply for U.S. citizenship)

N-400 – Naturalization (to become a U.S. citizen)

N-565 – Replace Naturalization/Citizenship Certificate

3 photos are required for the following forms:

I-698 – Temporary Resident's application under the 1987 Legalization Progra for permanent resident status — file 1 photo for your application, and bring other 2 with you to your interview

N-600K – To apply for U.S. citizenship for foreign-born child residing abroad with U.S. citizen parent

4 photos are required for the following forms:

I-817 – To apply for Family Unity Benefits

I-881 – NACARA — suspension of deportation or special rule cancellation

File the following with your photos and of others as shown bel

I-129F – Fiancé(e) Petition — file with 1 photo of you + 1 photo of fiancé(

I-130 – Relative petition — if filing for your husband or wife, file with 1 ph of you + 1 photo of your husband or wife

I-589 – Asylum — file with 1 photo of you + 1 photo of each family memb listed in Part A. II that you are including in your application

I-730 – Relative petition filed by a person granted Asylum or Refugee status file with 1 photo of the family member for whom you are filing the I-730

I-914 – 'T' nonimmigrant status — file with 3 photos of you + 3 photos of each immediate family member for which you file an I-914A supplement

All photos must be of just the person. Where more than one photo is required, all photos of person must be identical. All photos must meet the specifications for full-frontal/passport

For more information, visit our website at www.uscis.gov, or call our customer service at 1 800 375 5283.

Common USCIS Acronyms and Abbreviations

The following list contains definitions for many of the acronyms and abbreviations found in the paperwork and resources you may come across during the naturalization process. (Courtesy of the USCIS website, www.uscis.gov.)

A
ACE   Accelerated Citizen Examination
ADIT   Alien Documentation, Identification, and Telecommunication System
A File   Basic Alien File (contains Alien number)
AILA   American Immigration Lawyers Association
ARC   Alien Registration Card (Green Card)
ASC   Application Support Center (Naturalization)
ASVI   Alien Status Verification Index

B
BCC   Border Crossing Card (Mexico)
BCIC   Border Crossing Identification Card (I-586)

BHRHA	Bureau of Human Rights and Humanitarian Affairs
BIA	Board of Immigration Appeals
BP	Border Patrol
BSC	Baltimore Service Center

C

CAP	Citizens Advisory Panel
CAP	Cuban Adjustment Program
CBOs	Community-Based Organizations
CBIC	Canadian Border Intelligence Center
CFR	Code of Federal Regulations
CIJ	Chief Immigration Judge
CIMT	Crimes Involving Moral Turpitude
CIS	Central Index System
CPS	Current Population Survey (Census)
CUSA	Citizenship U.S.A.

D

DDP	Detention and Deportation Program
DED	Deferred Enforced Departure
DFS	Designated Fingerprint Service
DOE	Date of Entry
DOL	Department of Labor
DOS	Department of State

E

EAD	Employment Authorization Document
EFOIA	Electronic Freedom of Information Act Initiative
EOIR	Executive Office for Immigration Review

F

FCC	Fingerprint Clearance Coordination Center
FD-258	Fingerprint Card
FLSA	Fair Labor Standard Act
FOIA/PA	Freedom of Information Act/Privacy Act
FRC	Federal Records Centers

G

GREEN CARD	Alien Registration Receipt Card (Form I-151 or I-551)

H

HRO	Human Resource Office

I

IA	Immigration Agent
IAO	Office of International Affairs
ICF	Immigration Card Facility (Arlington, TX)

IDENT	Automated Fingerprint Identification System
IDP	In District Processing
IE	Immigration Examiner
II	Immigration Inspector
IIO	Immigration Information Officer
IIRIRA	Illegal Immigration Reform and Immigrant Responsibility Act
IJ	Immigration Judge
INA	Immigration and Nationality Act
IO	Immigration Officer
IRCA	Immigration Reform and Control Act of 1986

L

LAPR	Lawfully Admitted for Permanent Residence
LAW	Legally Authorized (or Admitted) Worker
LPR	Lawful Permanent Resident
LULAC	League of United Latin American Citizens

M

MIRP	Mexican Interior Repatriation Program

N

NACS	Naturalization Automated Casework System
NATZ	Naturalization
NGOs	Non-Governmental Organizations
NINSC	National INS Council
NIV	Non-Immigrant Visa
NRC	National Records Center
NSC	Nebraska Service Center (Lincoln)
NTA	Notice to Appear
NVC	National Visa Center (Department of State)

O

OIL	Office of Immigration Litigation
ONO	Office of Naturalization Operations

P

PHS	Public Health Services
POE	Port-of-Entry
PRC	Permanent Resident Card

R

RTD	Refugee Travel Document

S

SAW	Special Agricultural Workers

SIO   Special Inquiry Officer (Immigration Judge)
SPC   Service Processing Center
SW   Southwest

T
TAPS   Telephone Application Processing System
TSC   Texas Service Center (Irving)
TRWOV   Transit Without Visa

U
UNHCR   United Nations High Commissioner for Refugees
USC   U.S. Citizen
USCS   United States Customs Service

V
VD   Voluntary Departure
VR   Voluntary Return
VSC   Vermont Service Center (St. Albans)
VWPP   Visa Waiver Pilot Program

W
WRO   Western Region Office (Laguna Niguel, CA)